Telephone: MOUntview 3343.

HIGHGATE LITERARY & SCIENTIFIC INSTITUTION

920
Woo

11, SOUTH GROVE, N.6.

8800

Time allowed FOURTEEN Days

Date Issued	Date Issued	Date Issued
30 JUL 1954		
20 SEP 1954		
25 OCT 1954		
18 NOV 1954		
12 MAR 1956		
11 MAY 1959		
16 MAR 1964		
28 MAY 1975		
8 MAY 1979		
22 MAY 1979		

3000.5.51

ON HOLIDAY AT LUCERNE, 1936

THE LAST YEARS OF HENRY J. WOOD

by

JESSIE WOOD

with a foreword by

SIR MALCOLM SARGENT

LONDON
VICTOR GOLLANCZ LTD
1954

Printed in Great Britain by
The Camelot Press Ltd., London and Southampton

INTRODUCTION

THIS VOLUME TAKES up the story of Sir Henry Wood's life at the point where his autobiography *My Life of Music* left off in 1938. There has long been a need to fill out that earlier volume with the closing chapters of the life story Henry himself began, and now, in the diamond jubilee year of the Promenade Concerts, the need is even more urgent.

After much heart-searching, I became convinced that there was no one better able than myself to continue his biography from the inside, continue in the spirit of the earlier autobiography, for throughout Henry's later years after the breakdown of his second marriage I never left his side unless illness or other unforeseen occurrence demanded me elsewhere, thus fulfilling a promise I made him when he recovered from his first seizure early in 1935. In spite of the horrible war years and the disappointments and frustration, those ten years were perhaps the happiest of his life.

There is really only one more point to stress—that no preference or unkindness in relating facts is indicated anywhere in this story when the names of artists and others are mentioned. Inevitably, in a career which blazed a shining trail across the musical life of the times, there are some omissions in an account of this kind. It cannot discuss every performer or business connection with whom Sir Henry came in contact. This is Henry's own story, and other names are incidental to the topic in his life which happens to be under comment or review.

FOREWORD

"LORD, LET ME know mine end" was the cry of the psalmist in tragic bewilderment; a cry which few dare utter, lest they receive an answer.

Given the choice of an ending many would ask for a peaceful retirement, forgetting that old age almost inevitably brings, if not "pains", certainly "aches", which do not grow more comfortable with their continuance.

The more enlightened would wish that they might "die in harness". This was granted to the late and well-beloved Henry J. Wood. For years he wore the harness of his profession and art so firmly strapped upon him that even his infrequent holidays did not free him from his Herculean task.

All young people should read "My Life of Music", a book which Wood wrote and misnamed. It should have been entitled "My Life *for* Music". He of all men had a mind with a single eye. For him "to live" was "to make music".

His book remains as a solemn warning to those who think that "to conduct" is to tread an easy road to a glamorous success; his incessant labours and endurance shout "Halt" to those less gifted or less patient, even before they set foot upon the roseate path of delusion.

This book of "The Last Years" is a moving testimony written by one whom he dearly loved, and who devoted herself to him in his latter years, and since his death has ever sought a rightful preservation of his memory.

It is the story of a man no longer youthful in body, but ever youthful in spirit, and continuing to the end to fight (sometimes against stupidity or indifference) for music, and for those who loved it.

Music needs no words. No words can express music's deepest feelings. But if Music could speak, of Henry J. Wood she would say, "Well done, thou good and faithful servant. Enter thou . . ."

MALCOLM SARGENT.

CONTENTS

ILLUSTRATIONS

Only those who, like myself, had to act as critics of London music fifty years ago can possibly appreciate what we owe to Henry Wood. Younger connoisseurs have heard and seen him conduct; but they have not suffered from his early contemporaries the pre-Richter conductors. And they do not know, and would not believe me if I told them, what the Promenade Concerts were like at Covent Garden in the eighteen-eighties. It was Wood who dragged British orchestral music alive out of that abyss. And after a lifework which would have staled and worn out anyone but Wood, when the Wireless gave him an audience of millions to play to, in the Albert Hall with a splendidly full band, he rose to the occasion and surpassed himself in performances which crowned him as a master of his art and the peer of the greatest of his European rivals

G. Bernard Shaw

New Year 1944.

CHAPTER 1

The Busy 'Thirties

IN 1935 SIR HENRY WOOD, overtired and dispirited, suffered a slight stroke after returning to London from a conducting engagement in Rome. He soon recovered, but it was a grim sign that the combined burden of his personal worries and exacting work for music threatened to undermine even his immense stamina which for a generation had helped to make him the dominating personality of English music.

The middle 1930s, like that time in 1895 when he had conducted the first Promenade Concert at Queen's Hall, was in many ways the end of an era.

When he raised his baton on the evening of 10 August 1895 for the first of the concerts that were to revolutionize British musical taste, the long tranquillity of Victorian England was already drawing towards its sunset. Soon the young promenaders were to be reading war dispatches from South Africa and mourning the death of a queen who had reigned as long as most people remembered. And, as the Promenade Concerts moved towards their first decade, the age of the hansom cab was giving way to that of the motor-car.

By 1935, when nature warned Henry that he could no longer afford to take his great strength and vitality for granted, an entirely new generation was making its way summer after summer to Queen's Hall for concerts that had become a part of London's living tradition. Outside the concert hall menacing signs were once more warning of turbulent times ahead, troubled years that would sweep into oblivion so much that was a familiar part of life's daily pattern. When the blow fell in 1939, plunging us into the second world war, the Promenade Concerts also came near to being swept away in the general destruction.

Not that I had much time for dark forebodings about such things in 1935. My first care was to restore Henry's vigour and serenity and enable him to build up his strength. The relaxation of a holiday in France and Belgium before the 1935 Promenade season worked wonders and as the days went on bright happiness brought him back from the pit. He became a gay, expansive young man of sixty-six.

Years of hard and diligent work for both of us followed. The orchestra and public found a change as soon as the 1935 Promenade Concerts began. His mood of renewed hope and a new vitality were apparent in his music. Already work was afoot for the 1936 Sheffield Festival, destined to be the last of that grand tradition—for war intervened and, like much of traditional and artistic value, the old glory has not yet returned.

Surrounded though he always was with people, he remained a lonely soul. Unless a new work was on his mind, as soon as he had cleared up his schedule for the day he immediately felt the need of a companion to fall in with his mood. "Let's go for a walk in the park." "Let's go to a theatre" or "Read to me", he would ask. If you responded readily, then Henry was full of a relaxed happiness and so very grateful.

After the 1936 Promenade season he gave a dinner to the B.B.C. orchestra at the Langham Hotel. He was not singling out one particular orchestra; it must be remembered that in those days only one orchestra played during the whole season. This entertainment was a fresh delight for him, evidence of the new freedom of spirit and self-assurance that had grown since his recovery from earlier constraints and the ill-health of 1935.

"I've waited twenty years to be able to do this," he told Mr. E. Gillegin, timpanist of the B.B.C. Symphony Orchestra. Similar happy parties followed in 1937 and 1938. They were joyous gatherings. One year, I cannot recall which, Mr. Hinchliffe, contra bassoon player, was the winner of a competition to guess the number of leaves on the head of a pineapple. His prize was one of Henry's canvases, a sketch in oils of a Belgian scene.

No one was happier or more free than Henry on these occasions. "I'm not going to play Brahms's chamber music to you! We are going to have some fun! Kenway and Young and other artists are going to amuse us," he told the orchestra. What a host he was, so sure of himself and so happy in those friendly 'off-the-record' meetings with musicians, and very specially delighted to welcome his old friend Mrs. Rosa Newmarch among other friends not of the orchestra.

Victor Gollancz, the publisher, was determined to produce Henry's *My Life of Music* in a one-volume edition and at a price which would make it available to the general public. This meant a great deal of whittling down of the original manuscript which I had laboriously recorded in long-hand—not possessing the slightest knowledge of shorthand (I had tried going to school to acquire the art of Mr. Pitman's language when I found it difficult to take down everything that Henry dictated, including pertinent asides which were always breaking into his line of thought, but it was just Greek to me). What a scramble that first version was! There were only old programmes and Henry's memory to consult, but what a memory it was! Picking up the programme of some concert of years ago, he could recall almost what an artist had said or remember some little musical comment made by himself or a member of the orchestra. I had had no experience of compiling a book such as he visualized, but with that driving force, that invincible and insistent urge behind me, I found myself able to write to his dictation after all.

Work on the book started at the Palace Hotel at Lucerne in 1936, sitting out on the balcony overlooking the Lake of Lucerne and directly facing the Villa Triebschen where Wagner composed the immortal *Siegfried Idyll*. Henry, full of *joie-de-vivre*, sat, with easel and canvas, all agog to paint Triebschen, at the same time giving a running commentary on what I had written from notes taken the previous evening as I read aloud to him. I can still see, as I look over the pages of his autobiography, those terrific baskets which the porters hated so much on the journey from England. They were filled with programmes and reference books, and certainly provided material for unlimited work.

But it was a joyous holiday, contributing further to Henry's growing vigour and self-reliance. He could have 'ticked me off' with complete impunity had he wanted to—but I soon discovered that he would have made a perfect diplomat, so artfully and stealthily did he approach any mistake that crept into my account. Days might pass after my reading to him the version I had made of his dictation and not a word would be said. Then, with a casual reference, he would gently recall my blunder or omission.

When *My Life of Music* was published, his friend Rosa Newmarch wrote commenting on how little of his personal life was described in the autobiography.

"Ah," Henry remarked on reading her letter, "I could

hardly write more about myself than work accomplished in the name of music."

The chapter dealing with the *St. Matthew Passion* was to him almost the *raison d'être* of the book. He felt most earnestly that a growing clamour for 'purist' presentation of Bach and Handel—though laudable and right under certain conditions—was misleading, and such performances gave quite a false demonstration to a public unversed in conditions ruling in Bach's day. More than that, he believed completely in his readings of Bach. Bach always begged for more strings and had he lived to-day he would surely have used the great modern organs, the great orchestras, the great choirs and the large concert halls. "Was he not a man of expansive temperament who would have used all the lovely wind and strings of the present day, and, further, was he not the father of twenty-one children?" Henry argued. "No flapdiddle human, this, whose only means of reproducing his musical thoughts was via the instruments at his command and under conditions prevailing in the eighteenth century."

Henry was fearless on this point, and once wrote a letter to the Press on a presentation of Handel's *Messiah* advertised to be a performance "as Handel wrote it".

"As a servant of the musical public I feel it my duty to point out that the recent correspondence in your columns on the restoration of Handel's original orchestration of *The Messiah* is apt to be misleading, as it does not make it clear that a performance under such conditions would necessarily be an historical presentation of the work. To the uninitiated it might even seem to suggest that the vast *Messiah* public has been filling our concert halls at any time in any season for the past fifty years and more to listen to a gigantic artistic error perpetrated upon them by charlatans.

"In considering the manner in which Handel's *Messiah* is to be presented it is obviously necessary to take into account the nature and scope of the performance. I am all for performances of the historical type, provided that, so far as may be possible, the exact conditions ruling at the time the work was written are reproduced. In the case of *The Messiah* this would mean the employment of a small orchestra of not more than forty players and of a pigmy choir of not more than twenty-eight singers, as the original edition demands. Musicians will always remember those wonderful 'historical' concerts given at the Brussels Conservatoire under the direction of Gavaert and perfectly prepared and interpreted by the professors of that institution. Indeed, I have always wished to repeat the experiment here in one of our smaller concert halls.

"But it is necessary to draw a line of demarcation between performances of this kind and those on the more generous scale to which the musical public of this country is accustomed. The additional accompaniments which Mozart was commissioned to write in 1789 are evidence of the rapid development of orchestral and choral conditions during the forty-eight years which had elapsed since *The Messiah* was completed, and 113 years later the late Professor Prout produced his edition, now generally in use and widely accepted as a skilful and scholarly piece of work, well suited to the needs of our modern choral societies.

"It is performances of this type, in which our great choirs combine with our leading orchestras, which have endeared *The Messiah* to public and singers alike and which have established the fine British choral tradition, to which we owe the glorious modern masterpieces of Stanford, Parry, Elgar, Vaughan Williams, Walton, etc."

Henry's viewpoint has since been borne out by some more recent public performances, including a Bach choral work at the Royal Albert Hall in which critics complained that the so-called "Bach orchestra was quite inaudible above the massed voices of the choir of about 400."

This brings to mind the recent 'tampering' with Handel's Organ Concerto during the Henry Wood Promenade Concerts. Henry certainly 'tampered' in the first instance by using a full orchestra in keeping with the organ as we know it to-day, believing that had Handel visualized this instrument and those of the modern orchestra he would have used every string, breath of wood wind, brass, etc., to strengthen his own personal reinforcement, in view of the way in which he extemporized at the organ to get more out of the music than the scores of those days made possible. A number of kindred souls came to the conclusion that the Handel-Wood concertos had far too great a following during the Promenade Concerts and determined to demonstrate their 'purism' by making a new arrangement. But that cultured, analytical note-writer, Hubert Foss, in the 1949 Promenade Concert programme blew their whole argument to the winds, for he claimed that the seventeen organ concertos are 'chamber music', and yet at the same time admitted that "Handel's music is largely to blame for the gradual trend towards *rodomontade* with large choruses and orchestras"! He agreed in his note that Sir Henry Wood's policy "brought the organ concertos into wide popularity at the Promenade Concerts," but continued, in a magnificent effort to beg the question on behalf of the 'purists', that in re-scoring for *modern* conditions *"nearer to that which Handel would have used* [Handel's score was for oboes and strings], strings and oboes are retained as in Handel's scoring," but flutes, bassoons, horns, trumpets and drums are allowed to intrude in this new version, although "clarinets and trombones are excluded as being *unsuited* to the period."

All this is so foolish, for it is certain that if Handel had written these great works to-day he would have put them on to the full orchestras available, as Henry Wood has done. A trend of our times seems to be: "This is success. Let's pull it asunder. Never build, much less if it's another man's success."

*   *   *

The Decca Record Company approached us in 1936 with plans for an ambitious series of recordings. As a result George Stratton undertook to bring into existence again the Queen's Hall Orchestra. Henry held the copyright of the title "Queen's Hall Orchestra" as a gift from Sir Edgar Speyer, but since the death of Robert Newman in 1927, when the B.B.C. took over the sponsorship of the 'Proms', Henry had not had his own orchestra. It was a loss he felt deeply, and he often said in his later years how he had missed that encouragement which might have overcome his inherent timidity in business affairs—and persuaded him to lay out the capital during the 1920s to ensure the existence and continuity of the Queen's Hall Orchestra which had been his own for thirty-two years during the life of Robert Newman.

This lack of his own orchestra was a serious deprivation. Not only did it impede his visionary aims of taking it abroad and curb the artistic flights ever present in his mind, but it also curtailed almost to extinction his recordings for H.M.V. and Columbia.

So the move by Decca was a source of deep joy to Henry. George Stratton collected a really fine orchestra which gave

Henry much artistic satisfaction and many wistful reflections of the days in 1927 when he had so much wished to retain his old orchestra under a management in which he could participate. The Decca records were excellent but were not, of course, of the same splendid quality of recording as those they produce nowadays. I have kept a complete set of unused records, both Decca and Columbia, which I hope the students of the Royal Academy of Music will one day hear.

The Decca recording studios are—or were, at any rate, in those days—next door to a hostelry thronged always with artists having meals during the intervals of recording-sessions. One day we had reserved a table for lunch with some members of the Queen's Hall Orchestra and as we were going to take our place a waitress anxiously intercepted Henry to ask his name.

"Henry Wood," Henry answered.

"Oh, you can't sit here. It's reserved for Sir Henry Hall!" came the reply, amid cheers and laughter.

Perhaps it was Mr. Louis Dreyfus who gave Henry the most pleasing task of this year by sponsoring the Sunday afternoon concerts at Queen's Hall with Henry's newly re-constituted Queen's Hall Orchestra. A season of some eight concerts was given in 1936-37 and the following season they were taken up by Harold Holt, who sponsored ten or twelve concerts. They did not attract the large audiences which had been customary in the days of Robert Newman and later Messrs. Chappell, but, as Henry said, it would possibly take some years to reawaken public interest in these Sunday concerts which had lapsed since the B.B.C. took over the Queen's Hall Orchestra in 1927. One of the outstanding events of the resumed Sunday concerts was the debut on 21 March 1937 of Ida Haendel in the Beethoven Violin Concerto.

A little girl in short dress and socks, just fourteen years of age, she made a great impression, and not only on the public, for even Henry's usually careful guard was lowered in avowed wonder and admiration. "Kreisler again if she proceeds as she has begun—that little excitable *tremolo* and that lovely quality," he exclaimed. He congratulated Harold Holt on the find, and to-day Ida is a great artist and a great favourite the world over.

The French composer Roussel died in 1936, as did Henry's good friend Glazounov. He paid homage to both in memorial concerts. Roussel, when he met Henry in a Paris restaurant once, told him that no one else in England played his works.

* * *

There were the usual provincial concerts in 1936—Liverpool, Manchester, Hull, Hastings, Torquay, Southport and other towns. Henry was delighted to direct an amateur orchestra for his old friend A. E. Matthews, formerly a member of the Queen's Hall Orchestra. He journeyed to Southport on several occasions in connection with this work and thoroughly enjoyed the enthusiasm of all concerned from the mayor to a poor old flautist who fainted during one of the concerts. Then to Bournemouth, Belfast and Huddersfield—travelling always up and down the country.

Visits to Huddersfield gave Henry the utmost satisfaction. Bach's B minor Mass is perhaps one of the hardest tests possible for a chorus but here was a chorus-master after his own heart—Herbert Bardgett. It was electrifying singing—noble, and revealing a deep understanding of the text applied to the art of singing.

A lecture on "The Gentle Art of Singing" at the City Temple in the autumn of 1936 was a tremendous success. Only one with such consummate knowledge of the subject could have

given so delightful and convincing a talk—almost unbelievable, too, on hearing that lecture to recall how Henry hated
making speeches. "Speechifying", he called it.

"Ah, my dear," he said when I taxed him on the
matter, "but this is a subject I know by rote. It is my life."
He loved singers, every one of them, including the bad or
passable, for he always cherished hopes of improvement. It
is noticeable that in 1934 fifty-five singers appeared during the
eight-week season of Promenade Concerts and it was a cause
of very great regret to Henry when gradually the number of
solo singers was cut down and they were almost eliminated
from the Proms through the policy of shortening the programmes.

During the 1936-37 Sunday afternoon concerts at Queen's
Hall Neville Chamberlain was a deeply interested member of
the audience, and it gave Henry much pleasure to lunch with
him at Downing Street and talk about music and its educational value. It was on one such occasion that Neville
Chamberlain reminded Henry of his 'profound advice', as he
called it, when Birmingham was considering the foundation
of a municipal orchestra. Henry had acted in an advisory
capacity, offering the great midland city not only artistic
guidance but help in such matters as personal requirements,
fees, etc.

The climax of 1936 for Henry was the Sheffield Festival.
This alone, with its twenty-one rehearsals, meant diligent
study and constant travel. Rachmaninoff's *The Bells* was a
favourite work of Henry's—if he ever had favourites, for
every work he undertook received the same respect and sincere approach. Rachmaninoff was delighted with the performance in which Isobel Baillie, Parry Jones and Harold Williams
were the soloists.

But favourites there were. I can definitely say that Bach's Brandenburg Concerto No. 6, especially the slow movement, was singled out as such. "If you are here, dear Jessie, when I pass on, please let me hear Brandenburg No. 6," he once said to me.

CHAPTER 2

Henry's Conducting Jubilee

RARELY DID HENRY allow himself any social indulgences. He preferred to find relaxation at home, reading poetry or the latest Paper of the Royal Institution (of which he was a member) and talking over future plans or painting. His reading was not in the novel category but had a scientific trend and ranged over nearly every subject from religion of every denomination to engineering, carpentry, astronomy and so forth. Naturally, no book about music failed to find a purchaser in Henry J. Wood. He never borrowed books. He found much time over the years for sketching in oils, and some sixty canvases remain in our house showing that he could have been equally distinguished in this art. Since his death in 1944 I have had these paintings photographed by an expert and they now form a beautifully bound volume dedicated to his memory.

At one period he wished some of the art galleries—such as those of Hull, Sheffield and Manchester—to accept one of his paintings, but he changed his mind when he found that the governing bodies of these galleries had little sympathy with music in their cities. That discovery was made after Henry had taken the trouble to visit the governors at Hull in an endeavour to obtain support for the Hull Amateur Orchestral Society. Later he made several suggestions regarding his pictures but eventually said to me:

"I leave it to you to decide. Just wait and see how they treat me when I am gone."

Quite recently at my luncheon table was a happy party of musicians and artists including Frank O. Salisbury. Frank Salisbury turned to Lord Horder, also among the guests, and, pointing to Henry's fine canvas depicting a view of the valley of Bettws-y-Coed, said: "You know, I've never seen a better picture in the Royal Academy."

Henry had a deep interest in musical education which found tangible expression in his visits to Stowe School with the London Philharmonic Orchestra. For many years, also, the Hull Philharmonic Orchestra, which was entirely amateur, had provided work of that pioneer spirit of adventure in music of which he never tired, though in 1938 it became obvious that he could no longer continue the strain of the ambitious programmes on which the Hull Committee almost insisted. Even with such enthusiastic amateur personnel they were too ambitious. To watch Henry's direction during rehearsals (two or three for each of the three annual concerts) was to watch, as it were, an anxiously donned cloak of hypnotism insisting on demands all these dear young—and some old—people could not possibly execute.

He was grieved to have to resign after some sixteen years of training and so sever ties which had become a treasured achievement of progress. But Basil Cameron was at hand to carry on Henry's work in Hull and Henry felt comforted and assured after his resignation that enthusiasm would prevail and musical education persist into a far future. It was therefore a happy meeting in April 1939 when the Hull Philharmonic Society presented Henry with an onyx cigarette box as a farewell present.

His love and loyalty to the students of the Royal Academy of Music had made his journeys to Hull an exacting time-table, for both preliminary rehearsals and concerts took place on Thursdays and, as Henry's senior orchestra at the Royal Academy met on Fridays at 2.30 p.m., he always cheerfully caught the early morning train back to London and rushed to the Academy. Mark Hambourg played at Hull on one occasion and on passing the night porter's callboard remarked: "It looks like Hindemith sounds!"

We had planned to visit Prague early in 1936, but a series of events forced Henry to cancel what would have been a delightful prospect, as it had been hoped that his old and dear friend Rosa Newmarch might accompany us. The death of King George V altered many plans and as Henry suffered an injury to his arm at this time the Prague concerts had to be cancelled.

Talking of these past plans and friendships recalls, too, Henry's devotion to the music of and personal friendship for the great Finnish composer Sibelius. It was a friendship Henry shared with Sir Granville Bantock and Rosa Newmarch. Rosa Newmarch's little book *Jean Sibelius, a Short Story of a Long Friendship* is a delightful memoir (it is a pity Rosa left us without a fuller and later edition of her books on Henry J. Wood and the Promenade Concerts). In 1937 Henry insisted on playing the seven Sibelius symphonies during the Promenade Concert season, and a 'Sibelius Night' figured in the programme this season for the first time. I recollect that a few months later a concert-giving organization announced that the seven Sibelius symphonies were to be heard *in one season for the first time*. "So much for my work during the Proms," said Henry. But Sibelius himself had telegraphed on hearing the 'Sibelius Night' at the Promenade Concert in September 1937:

"My felicitations to your great success with my works.

The concert was for me unforgettable. With cordial thanks and greetings—Sibelius."

When in 1939 it was rumoured that Sibelius's Symphony No. 8 was on the way—that, indeed, agreement had been reached regarding its first performance—Henry wrote to Sibelius at once and received the following reply:

"24 July 1939.

"My dear friend Sir Henry,

"Many thanks for your kind letter of July 3rd which, unfortunately, I have not been able to answer before. I was very glad to receive a message from you once again.

"Nothing could be dearer to me than to know that my Eighth Symphony would be performed by you, to whom I am so much indebted, and I would be delighted to comply with your request.

"The fact is, however, that I am not yet able to tell you when the new work, which has already been so much discussed, can be produced. So let's wait and see!

"With friendship and admiration,

"Always yours,

"Jean Sibelius."

Henry was delighted to receive the great man's daughter when she visited us in 1938 bringing many messages from her father.

That year, 1938, was a time of many festivals: Eastbourne, Hastings, Bath, The Three Valleys, Morecambe, Newtown, Glasgow and Torquay among others. It was also Henry's jubilee as a professional conductor. What a joy it was for him to prepare under ideal conditions the great Mahler Symphony

No. 8, performed at Queen's Hall in February at a B.B.C. symphony concert. It involved many weeks of careful work, marking every nuance, every detail, every breath-mark in the chorus parts.

Henry had a great admiration for Bruno Walter's work, and I remember when he was rehearsing the Mahler Symphony No. 8 in 1937 he remarked:

"How I wish we could get Bruno Walter to do this great work. He would give us the true Mahler." Walter had studied under Mahler himself in Vienna.

In 1948 the Henry Wood Concert Society, of which I am chairman, invited Bruno Walter to come to England to direct Mahler's Symphony No. 8—called the 'Symphony of a Thousand', so large are the forces of orchestra, choir and soloists needed for this work. Unfortunately Dr. Walter was too unwell to come to London that season as announced and Sir Adrian Boult directed it on 10 February 1948 in his stead, but Walter came to us in 1949 to direct Mahler's Second Symphony, *The Resurrection*. This was of particular interest, as Henry had had it down for a first performance in England in 1911 at the Birmingham Festival. It was not performed on that occasion, as Mahler had died just previously and he was to have directed his own work. The Henry Wood Concert Society's performance under Bruno Walter's direction, with the B.B.C. Symphony Orchestra and Chorus and Dora Van Doorn and Kathleen Ferrier as soloists is a glorious memory which also implemented a wish expressed by Henry in 1911 and again in 1937. How well I remember the many occasions during the war when familiar programmes of the classical repertoire were persistently demanded by managements and Henry yearned for the opportunity to perform lesser known works.

The intensive study on the Mahler symphony in 1938 recalls

the marvel of Henry's immaculate preparation for the musical festivals at Norwich, Birmingham, Sheffield and elsewhere. His careful thought for the accompanist at the piano for chorus rehearsals; his knowledge of singing which made him aware of the strain on the amateur voice in such works as the Beethoven Choral Symphony; his capacity for knowing in advance just where the tenors will shriek in their effort to dominate the volume of the voices of easier range; all this was part of the genius with which he approached these festivals and which lay behind those fine, polished performances that the public applauded, often without the least realization of the work that had been put into them.

The Beethoven Choral Symphony, for instance, was always rehearsed a tone down, and Henry even went to the trouble of having a transposed vocal score for the accompanist, aware as he was that not all provincial piano accompanists transposed at a moment's request without blunders—a nerve-wracking business at the best of times. Henry always marked a master copy of the vocal score for every choral conductor, perhaps a year or more in advance of the date of the festival! Some people are inclined to disparage "old Wood's blue pencil". But ask the chorus-masters and their singers! They will tell you how much easier it was to approach the final rehearsals of a work knowing that every breath-mark had been noted well in advance and, moreover, that what had once been marked in the vocal score did not vary when Henry arrived to take over the rehearsals. Such preparation goes back to Henry's very early days.

Discipline? Well, if correct preparation for presenting a choir to the public in a great choral work is to be called discipline (and nothing more) then—as Walford Davies said when introducing Henry to hundreds of Welsh choral singers before a rehearsal for one of the Three Valleys festivals—Henry Wood certainly was a disciplinarian. Sir Walford told his singers: "We've had many conductors here, and recently that fine musician Malcolm Sargent. Now we have here with us the disciplinarian Sir Henry Wood."

In practice, 'discipline' worked out like this: when Henry was to direct a choir drawn from several choral societies, as at Kendal, The Three Valleys or the Crystal Palace, he would send those marked vocal scores to every chorus-master. Not only would every breath- and expression-mark be noted, but he would include instructions on rising and sitting, the exact placing of the chorus and orchestra and the general layout. He would also take a rehearsal with every contingent co-operating in the final amalgamated event.

In the annotated vocal scores even the enunciation would be dealt with and such careful reminders be included as: "It is here the tenors flatten" or "It is here the contraltos get breath-y tone". Henry would also indicate where there might be variation in beat: "I beat six (or whatever it might be) in a bar here" and so on. Every chorus-master thus received precise indications so that when the amalgamated rehearsals arrived the singers were accustomed to the beat and other important details and time was not wasted in lessons in phrasing and expression. Band parts would also be carefully marked and Henry would have printed at his own expense slips to be given to every choralist. For Bach's B minor Mass, for instance, printed directions for the singers covered some sixteen to twenty-five pages.

Henry provided leaflets for such works as Dvorak's *Stabat Mater*, Beethoven's *Missa Solennis*, the Bach *Magnificat*, Palestrina's *Lamentation*, Verdi's *Requiem*, Bach's *St. Matthew Passion*, Bach's *Phoebus and Pan*, Elgar's *King Olaf*, Brahms's *German*

Requiem and all choral work. By his phonetic spelling methods he made the work of singing an unknown tongue much easier for a chorus.

At the end of each booklet is printed a section entitled "For Daily Practice", comprising various difficult passages, expression-marks, breath-marks and phonetic spelling of the foreign text.

Henry's treatise *The Gentle Art of Singing* (published by the Oxford University Press in four volumes) is another example of his intense attention to detail backed by utter sincerity and integrity. He evinced the same concern in the layout of his orchestra for a particular work, whether orchestral or choral with orchestra. A diagram was always given to the orchestral attendant to avoid any possibility of error. The ever-faithful Edgar Mays and Mr. Fussell (both B.B.C. attendants) appreciated Henry's unstinted assistance in this way, just as orchestral managers were grateful for his accurate rehearsal timing. If Henry called a soloist at a given time, he was ready at that time.

Discipline? Was it not rather a real and deep knowledge of the scores he dealt with; and more, of understanding just how much time must be given to a certain work or particular passages of a certain work? And the solo artist always did receive adequate time, not only for a run-through but for polishing up shaky points. And there always was a piano rehearsal on a date preceding the concert rehearsal with the orchestra.

"It is Mr. so-and-so this morning. He's always fidgety. I must allow him plenty of time," Henry would say as he planned his rehearsal list for the day. How all these dear artists, as he used to call them, must have missed him.

Henry's sixty-ninth birthday, on 3 March 1938, was a red-

SIR HENRY'S FATHER IN 1898

SIR HENRY'S MOTHER ON HER WEDDING DAY

PRINCESS OLGA AT THE TIME OF HER WEDDING

HENRY WOOD AT THE AGE OF TWENTY-SIX

letter day. We were at the Alexandra Palace for a television rehearsal in the early morning, Henry brimming over with interest at the prospect of experiencing something new and scientific. All the same, he hated the strong lights and heat and was quite glad when it was all over. In fact, he was looking forward to shopping and later to a birthday dinner, so that even to be televised for the first time took second place when he thought of the free hours ahead. He was not too pleased, however, when I told him I hoped he would enjoy lunching with Flora and Ralph Lion at their studio.

"Whatever for? I want to walk; let's go into Bond Street and buy something!" he exclaimed. Henry's shopping usually resulted in a jar of preserved ginger!!

But Flora Lion had painted my portrait for his birthday present. It was to be a surprise, an expressed wish fulfilled, all unknown to him until this moment.

I shall always remember his expression of sheer delight when he turned round in the studio and saw Flora's fine work. "Nothing," he said, "could have given me more happiness and comfort than this. I have wanted one so much." In after years he would, whenever possible, have his desk with the portrait above it in the picture whenever any Press photographers came along. As the photographers prepared their cameras, Henry would plant himself firmly beside the desk and endeavour to have the picture taken in that attitude.

On 6 March 1938 he directed Yehudi Menuhin in three violin concertos with the London Philharmonic Orchestra at the Royal Albert Hall, and that same evening he directed a B.B.C. studio concert with Ida Haendel playing the Mendelssohn violin concerto. To conduct these two great young virtuosi—Yehudi twenty-one years old and little Ida just over fourteen—in one day was an experience Henry never forgot, and when artists such as these crossed his path he followed their career watchfully; they were his 'children in music'.

At this time we were busy cutting the manuscript of *My Life of Music* so that Victor Gollancz could produce it at a price suitable for the more general public. Henry found it a strain, for this pressing work coincided with preparations for *The Dream of Gerontius*, and with so many calls on his attention he could not work at ease. But before long he was able to concentrate entirely on his music once more. The Bach *St. Matthew Passion*, *The Dream of Gerontius* and *Parsifal* (concert version) had a special place in his heart among choral works.

Henry discovered in 1938, as at the 1936 Sheffield Festival, that the deputy question in orchestras was still unsolved and was still like a running sore that refuses to heal, draining the strength of English orchestras. Right back in 1904 this same problem provoked one of those crises that sometimes blow up in orchestral life, leading—as in this case—to mingled frustration and fruitlessness. Henry at Queen's Hall had been growing increasingly concerned at the habit of orchestral musicians of taking engagements elsewhere, then calmly engaging deputies to perform for them at their regular assignment with the orchestra to which they belonged. Henry would toil to bring his team to the required standard at rehearsal, working over the awkward passages and anticipating the pitfalls until the orchestra reached concert pitch. Hours later, as the public gathered to hear the performance, Henry would sometimes find himself conducting another set of players altogether, because many of those he had trained had taken engagements elsewhere and paid deputies to sit behind their instruments in the regular orchestra.

The abuses of the system are obvious, and in 1904 Robert

Newman, at Henry's behest, advised the musicians of the Queen's Hall Orchestra that he would no longer countenance deputies in the orchestra. Several members 'walked out', eventually banding themselves into the London Symphony Orchestra and vowing never again to be directed by Henry Wood. It amused Henry, but also delighted him, that their attitude resulted in the London Symphony Orchestra going outside England for their conductors. During their first season London was fortunate enough to welcome Nikisch, Steinbach, Colonne and others—and the L.S.O. had no greater enthusiast and admirer than Henry Wood for their enterprise.

In 1938, when greeting the orchestra for a concert at the Glasgow Exhibition, Henry was confronted by a mere smattering of the regular personnel of the L.S.O. Stepping on to the rostrum, he remarked quite frankly that apparently the policy which had resulted in the formation of the orchestra in 1904 was still in operation—and he could not understand how the L.S.O. came to be playing in Glasgow and at a concert announced in London for the same day. As Henry addressed the orchestra, he had no idea that the Glasgow manager was also listening! George Stratton, the leader of the orchestra, and some other principals were there, but the cat was out of the bag about those deputies! The Glasgow management were not pleased.

Not much later, by a twist of fate, the London Symphony Orchestra was only too eager to draw on the skill and reputation of Henry Wood when the supply of foreign conductors dried up in 1939-40 and our music stood still as it awaited the extinction Hitler had promised this country. Henry was the first to come to the rescue, and a footnote in the programme of a concert at Queen's Hall given by the L.S.O. at this time declares:

"The opening of the 1939-40 season was a critical one, and the annals of the London Symphony Orchestra bear witness to the generous action of Sir Henry Wood in coming to the assistance of the orchestra when so many conductors of international reputation were unavailable. The first concert under wartime conditions was given early in October 1939, at a time when all other organizations were eagerly awaiting such a courageous venture. As a result of this initiative there was a rapid revival of all musical activities throughout London and the provinces."

A vivid memory of the Bournemouth Musical Festival of 1938 was of Dame Ethel Smyth. Henry had arranged to meet her for a chat over tea at the hotel where we were staying. When in a public room, Henry always tucked himself into a quiet corner as far out of sight as possible. On this occasion the large lounge was full of people and noise. Suddenly, down the few steps came Dame Ethel, lifting her tricorn hat from her head and dumping it on again at a different angle, and exclaiming loudly:

"Where is Henry Wood? I've come to see Henry Wood."

All eyes sought Henry, who, fearful of public demonstrations, popped his head round the column or palm behind which he was sitting.

"Ah! There you are! Do you believe in women in orchestras, Henry?" she continued, all the time advancing as only Dame Ethel could, quite oblivious of having caused any sensation. "They tell me over there that they do not employ women, it's too cold for them to play out of doors." The last few words were lost to the wide-eyed crowd, for we had by then piloted her to our hide-out.

Actually she knew all the time that Henry would support her plea and had come on the very day on which he was con-

ducting the festival. Henry agreed that he liked women in
orchestras; had he not opened the ranks to them years ago
and welcomed Marie Wilson as leader of the B.B.C. Symphony Orchestra in 1936 in the Promenade Concert seasons
at Queen's Hall? Yes, he promised her, he would talk to the
management, but at that moment the arrival of Stravinsky
with his son saved further parley. We were later to see much
of Dame Ethel in a warm friendship and a rather fruitless
effort to save the British Women's Symphony Orchestra. We
often visited her at Woking, enjoying great fun and a feast
of reminiscences, for although she was quite deaf she never
let go—never became dull but was always alive and full of
spirit.

It was at this time that Henry came to know the Russian
ambassador, Mr. Maisky, and his wife who was an accomplished musician. Over the years we had many pleasurable
meetings, not least of which was a wartime luncheon attended
by Mr. and Mrs. Anthony Eden, Lord and Lady Woolton,
Mr. Oliver Lyttelton, Baron E. de Cartier de Marchienne
(the Belgian ambassador), and poor Leslie Howard, who was
killed in a flying accident very soon afterwards. During the
war there can hardly have been a meal so delightful and so
elegantly served as this private embassy lunch. Mrs. Maisky,
with a captivating smile, looked over the table to Lord
Woolton, sitting on my left, and remarked:

"You are taking notice, are you not, Lord Woolton, that
so far we have not disobeyed your orders? Do you not like
our margarine patted up in this manner?" Lord Woolton, of
course, was Minister of Food at the time.

Henry was troubled later when he had to disappoint his old
friend Benno Moseiwitsch, whose idea it was to get the Russian
embassy to patronize the Rachmaninoff tribute concert.

Maisky was very sympathetic, but that was all. He probably had to think first of his own career and the borders which a Soviet ambassador dare not cross. Benno Moiseiwitsch had, however, done wonderful work for Mrs. Churchill's "Aid to Russia Fund", subscribing, I believe, several thousand pounds through his own recitals all over the country and this silent refusal to honour Rachmaninoff (a scion of the old Russian régime) hurt Benno deeply. Henry, too, who felt that Rachmaninoff's music, and the man himself, had done so much to vindicate the grand tradition, past and present, of Russia's musical and artistic genius, shared Benno's regrets. Rachmaninoff had died on 28 March this year and his protégé and friend Benno had conceived the idea of this tribute to his memory, which would at the same time help Mrs. Churchill's fund. So on 7 June the concert took place before a crowded Royal Albert Hall. Benno played the three concertos with the London Symphony Orchestra. Henry found it a strain so soon after his illness, for he revered Rachmaninoff and his work and felt the emotional stress. A happy ending came with Mrs. Churchill's charming words of thanks during her supper party after the concert. Of course both Benno and Henry gave their services.

But to return to 1938. Henry had already agreed to direct the Three Valleys Music Festival in the closing days of May that year when another request had come from Sir Walford Davies:

> "High Meadow,
> "Cookham Dean,
> "Maidenhead,
> "10 October 1937

"My Dear Henry,
   "*Again Wanted!!*
"Yet another Welsh Musical Festival, a one-day Festival

also doing the Matthew Passion, same selection, same edition (so that makes it easier)—wants Sir Henry to be their conductor, in the heart-and-soul sense of that word. The date is May 12th, the place is Newtown, Montgomeryshire (Shrewsbury station where a car meets you).

"It is possible to put May 19th if May 12th does not suit you. We started the Montgomeryshire Festival 14 years ago, and in 1923 I conducted the Matthew Passion. They've never done it since—now great keenness to have you do it. Do say a heavenly Yes to this also. You will be doing a good deed and a glorious duty,

"Yours,
"Walford."

Henry read the letter, and remarked drily: "It's too honeyed, but if Wally-Wally (whether this was Henry's or a customary nickname I do not know) thinks I am going to have him 'at the piano' extemporizing he's mistaken. I'll get a Hammond organ and engage a special organist."

Henry disliked this very mangled version of the *St. Matthew Passion* which Sir Walford proposed, but apparently it had already been put into rehearsal both for Newtown and the Three Valleys Festivals and he felt it safer to accept it. Mr. Charles Clements took charge of the Hammond organ and the *continuo*.

Although Henry did not take Sir Walford's honeyed letter too literally, it gave him satisfaction as a gesture towards repairing a coolness which had grown up between the two some time earlier, when Henry had rebuked Sir Walford for interfering in his private affairs—about which Sir Walford was in any case singularly ill-informed.

The Newtown Festival was a marked success in its fifteenth

year. Sir Walford Davies travelled back with us the following day, as usual full of anecdotes and over-brimming emotion in relation to the forthcoming Three Valleys Festival. It was pleasurable, too, to have him thank me for looking after 'our Henry' so well! The Three Valleys concerts took place in that vast pavilion at Mountain Ash in which sixteen choirs amalgamated, with the Welsh Symphony Orchestra led by W. H. Reed, M.V.O. Again the *St. Matthew Passion* and *Samson* filled two days, while the third was devoted to Vaughan Williams's lovely *Toward the Unknown Region*.

Lord Horder was not happy about Henry's health at this time and advised me to follow a go-slow policy, with more free days and no speeches. Free days were a problem, for if a clean leaf appeared in his diary Henry at once plunged into fresh study, working anew possibly on *Gerontius*, *Parsifal* or the *St. Matthew Passion*; or perhaps new compositions in readiness for the Promenade Concerts. The only chance of real rest was for me to say I felt tired and plead for a few days out of London, at which Henry, immediately concerned, would reply: "At once, dear. Where shall we go?"

The opportunity for one such break came, and we stayed with my son-in-law at Mayfield. For two weeks, being in the neighbourhood, we were able to attend some of the lovely productions at Glyndebourne. Henry came home refreshed and so buoyant that anxiety about his health was allayed for the moment. Only for the moment, however; I knew my Henry.

At this time he agreed to become president of the Thermionic Club, which had its delightful headquarters near the Langham Hotel. For once—as I had much work to catch up on, and I felt Henry was safely guarded in the hands of Leslie Boosey and many friends—I did not go to the meeting marking his installation as president. I reminded him, however, that he would have to make an opening speech.

Off he went, and, to my inquiry on his return, "What did you say, how did it go?" he replied:

"I couldn't think what to say, it was so hot and crowded. Then my eye caught sight of a dart-board and I propounded at length on the fun of the game."

"But you don't really play darts!" I exclaimed.

Next morning the Press told the story, however, and we were showered with invitations from would-be hosts at darts matches, a particularly insistent club being that of the London bus drivers! How we laughed over it all!

The year 1938 was Henry's golden jubilee as a professional conductor. He had received his first fee in 1888 in connection with the opening concert of the seventh season of the All Saints' Choral Society, Clapton, at which Sir G. A. Macfarren's cantata *May Day* was performed in his memory (Sir George had been president of the society, and died on 1 October 1887). I drew Henry's attention to this fiftieth anniversary one day as I was scanning the pages of a book of Press cuttings which his father had carefully kept from the time of young Henry's very early public appearances as an organist, composer and conductor.

Henry's immediate interest in the date dissolved into nostalgic memories of the enthusiasm evinced by the choral singers of the Clapton and many other choral organizations with which he had been associated in those very early days and with whom he had taught himself the art of conducting.

I told Parry Jones, some time in 1937, of the conducting jubilee, and he, with John Tillett, became the leading spirits in a movement to mark it in a special manner.

A committee, headed by Robert (later Sir Robert) Mayer,

with Sir Hugh Allen, Sir James Jeans, Lord Horder, Dr. (later Sir) George Dyson, Professor (later Sir) Stanley Marchant, Sir Landon Ronald and Baron Frederic d'Erlanger, was formed to pay tribute to Henry. Sir Landon Ronald died shortly before the concert. It was a sad blow to Henry for they were old and staunch friends. Latterly, during Landon's long illness, we had run in to see him most days when Henry was not in the provinces. A more than devoted regard for Landon's cultured musicianship drew these two even nearer in Henry's hope that his friend would recover.

A concert was proposed, and Henry decided that whatever funds were collected or derived from it should go to found beds in London hospitals for orchestral musicians. Sir Hugh Allen was perhaps the most prominent in furthering the scheme and, as I pen these lines, with the hollow walls of Queen's Hall still a monument to Hitler's Germany, it is appropriate to quote Sir Hugh's view on this jubilee. "Queen's Hall should be renamed Wood's Hall, or some such title, to remind future musicians of what you accomplished," he wrote to Henry.

Once Henry's interest in the proposal was aroused, he entered into the planning with his usual enthusiasm. He was much concerned that if he suggested one soloist, he would find himself obliged to give the arena of the Albert Hall over to grand pianos and their attendant artists. Finally he wrote to Rachmaninoff, and Rachmaninoff replied "Yes."

The B.B.C. generously gave the services of their symphony orchestra, and the L.S.O. and the L.P.O. joined forces, providing an orchestra of over 200 players. Although it had been hoped that the committee could have announced the concert for St. Cecilia's Day (22 November), it had to be fixed for 5 October to fit in with Rachmaninoff's commitments.

Rachmaninoff made the journey to England for this concert alone, returning to America the next day. It was a great gesture, and Henry felt the honour deeply.

In March 1936 Rachmaninoff had lunched with us in our home in Elsworthy Road. There were other guests and, of course, our Scottie, Michael. Michael always had his chair at the table—not to be fed, but to take his place with the company. He sat upright, supporting himself with his front paws on the edge of the table, looking on. He had an "I'm one of the party" interest in all the proceedings. His head would move in the direction of each speaker.

For a long time Rachmaninoff did not appear to notice the dog. Then he suddenly exclaimed:

"Where did you get your Michael? He is human. I have bought a Scottie for my daughter, but I have never seen anything so intelligent as your Michael."

Alas! when Rachmaninoff came to see us again in March 1938 he was horrified to see a change in our friend. "Michael is going to die," he told us, and die our little dog did on 22 April. Eleven years of sweet friendship were over. Henry was in Cardiff then.

It was the first time in years that Henry had been left to travel alone, but we both agreed that I could not leave our dear friend when he was so ill. When Henry returned from South Wales he autographed several photographs of Michael with the inscription "Our dear Michael, Henry J. Wood, April 22nd, 1938". The photographs were framed and Henry placed one in every room we used.

The programme for the concert was reviewed with the jubilee committee. Of course there must be a chorus and singer, for singers were perhaps Henry's real love. Look back over Promenade Concert programmes and note, down the years, how carefully he provided time to give singers a chance to show what they could do: a good longish aria in the first half of the programme and solos with pianoforte accompaniment in the second.

He deplored the continually decreasing time given to them in later years. He argued that it was because of this policy that public interest had waned. And so "Singers", as many as could be gathered round him for this jubilee night, was his excited request. He knew he would get his own way on this occasion.

The outcome of his wish was Dr. Vaughan Williams's *Serenade to Music*. It required sixteen solo singers and a full orchestra. In the first sketch Dr. Vaughan Williams has inscribed:

"*Serenade to Music* composed for, and dedicated to, Sir Henry Wood on the occasion of his jubilee, in grateful recognition of his great services to music."

He added:

"This serenade will (it is hoped) be performed for the first time on October 5, 1938, when the singers will be Isobel Baillie, Stiles-Allen, Elsie Suddaby, Eva Turner, Margaret Balfour, Muriel Brunskill, Astra Desmond, Mary Jarred, Parry Jones, Heddle Nash, Frank Titterton, Walter Widdop, Norman Allin, Keith Falkner, Roy Henderson, Harold Williams. If subsequent performances of this work take place and the above singers (indicated by their initials in the score) are not available, other singers will have to take their places, or the solo parts may be sung in chorus. —V. W."

Henry said, and we are all agreed, that it is impossible to describe the sheer beauty of this work. It is of heaven, and it moved Henry to tears of emotion. No words could have honoured Henry Wood as did *Serenade to Music*, and it made him humbly grateful. During the first rehearsal the singers were so moved that their lips seemed unable to articulate. Each part had been written especially for that particular singer, each of Vaughan Williams's choice. The performance made a profound impression and it was received with cheers from the packed Albert Hall.

Henry subsequently wanted to repeat it more frequently but it is a costly business to provide sixteen solo singers and, although it has of course been performed many times with the solo voices, it has also been done with a small choir or with the B.B.C. singers. No matter how well these chorus voices have sung, the charm of the work is lost, as its elusive beauty is emphasized by the different qualities and timbre of the solo voices.

Later Henry suggested that it would be a good idea to make an orchestral arrangement. Vaughan Williams agreed, thus making a most valuable contribution to the orchestral repertoire. Henry gave the first performance of the orchestral version on 10 February 1940 with the London Symphony Orchestra at Queen's Hall. Vaughan Williams asked Henry to designate a cause to receive the royalties of the work—and so all the royalties are dedicated to the British Musicians' Pension Society, to swell the fund provided to assist the family when a musician is in one of the Henry Wood beds in London hospitals. The royalties amount to a goodly sum annually.

Rachmaninoff was in our box during the performance of *Serenade to Music*. His concerto having been played in the first half of the concert, he sat in the box to listen to the rest of the evening's music. His eyes filled with tears and, going to the back of the box, he sat down, declaring: "I feel ill, I feel sick, I think I must go home."

Weingartner, sitting by my side, turned round in that stiff collar—the hallmark of his elegance—and exclaimed: "I hope he won't be sick!"

Rachmaninoff told Henry afterwards that he had never before been so emotionally moved by music. Of his own reception that night, when he played his Concerto No. 2 in C minor, he said that nowhere in the world had the public greeted him so uproariously. The Albert Hall audience clamoured and shouted, shouted and clamoured, while Rachmaninoff travelled up and down that dreadful slope from the artists' room to the platform. The wildest excitement captured both orchestra and audience when these two dear men—Rachmaninoff and Henry—both obviously deeply moved, shook hands again and again. Rachmaninoff had received a rare ovation and it was a rare moment; for not only had the composer interpreted with a serene mastery his favourite concerto but he had on the rostrum the man who believed in that work. Henry revered Rachmaninoff.

Every player, too, entered into the spiritual and festival moment which they shared with Henry that night. Underneath all the stories about stern discipline, at heart the older orchestral player loved 'Henry J.', while the younger generation of orchestral musicians know, or should know, that they owe to his tireless efforts their status to-day. All together paid homage that unforgettable night.

Possibly the most touching tribute presented to Henry was a laurel wreath sent from South Africa by the City of Cape Town Municipal Orchestra, to mark Henry's conducting jubilee. The conductor of the Cape Town orchestra, William J.

Pickerill (who has since died), sent greeting by special envoy in the person of Miss Clark, who travelled to England for the purpose. The day following London's tribute the Cape Town orchestra gave a concert which included Rachmaninoff's Symphony No. 2. In the programme was a photograph of Henry, with the inscription:

"In Homage——Sir Henry J. Wood, D.Mus., F.R.A.M.
"1889——Jubilee Concert——1938
"It is fifty years since Sir Henry Wood made his first public appearance as a conductor. Last night's Jubilee Concert at the Royal Albert Hall, London, celebrated this stage in his wonderful career of music-making."

It was a great day—Henry's day—just as his friends had wished and planned. We gave a luncheon at which the solo singers were present, together with other colleagues. Later, at our reception after the concert, everybody came to shake Henry by the hand. He simply revelled in it and made a 'schoolboy' speech, a friendly and intimate gesture to his friends of music. The sixteen solo singers presented him with a pair of beautiful ivory brushes and gave me a most charming handbag. There were no long speeches, but I was kept busy for many days answering the letters from friends known and unknown. Many of these letters remain, with much other musical data and documentary material for a future biographer.

If any moment of regret remained in Henry's memory of the preceding months, while Robert Mayer and his committee were so jealously building up this conducting jubilee tribute, it was the difficulty of meeting the wishes of the B.B.C. (of which Henry had eventually to be told) who naturally wished to broadcast Rachmaninoff. At one stage it was suggested that unless Rachmaninoff allowed himself to be broadcast the B.B.C. might conceivably withdraw from the jubilee tribute. It was comforting for me to be able to shoulder all these preliminary discussions and so keep Henry free from frustration at such a time. It was wonderful to feel his calm, unruffled trust and faith that all was moving along serenely towards his great day—and music's great reward. Not until Rachmaninoff came to London in March 1938 could we hope to press the requests, almost the demands, made by the B.B.C. Letters failed to move Rachmaninoff. So we gave a luncheon at our home on 30 March for him to meet the members of the committee and representatives of the B.B.C.

Everyone present did all they could to persuade him. Sir Hugh Allen was most eloquent and the B.B.C. expressed readiness to give a very large sum to the jubilee fund for the privilege. But Rachmaninoff was adamant—and, in fact, he never was heard 'live' on the air.

Looking round the table, as everyone tried to overcome his objections to broadcasting, Rachmaninoff said:

"No, no, I will never do that."

Then he added morosely: "But I expect they will put on a record of the concerto while I play in the Albert Hall."

"Oh, no!" Henry told him. "We don't do that kind of thing in this country."

And there it was. Rachmaninoff just wouldn't budge.

Part of the concert had to be cut from the broadcast in consequence and although it all ended comfortably poor old Henry felt sorry that the great day should have suffered even a surface ruffle with the B.B.C.

Before the jubilee lunch, Rachmaninoff had come to see Henry on two occasions that month in connection with his

Third Symphony. He had written from New York on 15 December 1937:

"My Dear Sir Henry,

"About ten days ago I read in the *New York Times* a letter from London where it was said that the first performance of my Third Symphony had received a very poor Press. This news afflicted me, of course, but when I read your kind letter of November 26 and found that you liked my new composition, I was very glad and forgot all my griefs. Thank you! I expect to meet you in London in the beginning of March and to have a talk with you about the symphony.

"With best wishes,
"I am sincerely,
"Rachmaninoff."

Henry replied in longhand:

"I was pleased to have your letter. Posted on the high seas it seems to indicate that you are returning to Switzerland for the festival season.

"I am playing your new symphony at Liverpool on March 22, at a B.B.C. studio broadcast on April 3, and am hoping to get it down in Hull on April 7. So if I can have a chat with you when you are here for your recital in March, I shall feel I have every point well in mind which will be of inestimable value to me.

"Yours,
"Henry J. Wood."

These two men were of a kind rarely found. Both full

of enthusiasm—'Rach' for his new baby, No. 3, and Henry full of very sincere appreciation of the new work. On each occasion they sat at the piano for a couple of hours or more, Henry sometimes beating out his instruction. The intense study put into that symphony, with the composer's intentions laid down, made it for Henry quite like a work of his own and one that he really loved.

After Henry had sent a statement of the results of the jubilee concert, Rachmaninoff wrote in July 1939:

"7 July 1939

"My Dear Sir Henry,

"Many thanks for sending me the statement of the results of the concert.

"I am delighted at the great success of the splendid work for which you are responsible. I am glad to know that you are repeating my Third Symphony with my favourite orchestra (B.B.C. Symphony Orchestra). I shall most certainly listen in to it.

"With best greetings,
"Rachmaninoff."

The concert produced some £9,000, and with the proceeds nine beds were endowed for musicians at London hospitals. The beds were endowed as follows—three at Charing Cross, two at Bart's., and one each at St. Mary's, University College, Westminster and Wembley Hospitals.

The money left over after endowing these beds went to the Henry Wood Fund within the British Musicians' Pension Society for the use of dependants when the beds were in use. The society graciously undertook to administer the scheme. I fear the beds have not been called upon as much as they could or should have been—perhaps because this thoughtfulness of Sir Henry towards his orchestral musicians is not sufficiently known or understood by musicians, and, alas! nationalization has swept aside such generosity into oblivion in a plethora of civil service doctoring.

CHAPTER 3

Early Years

DURING THE TUMULTUOUS acclaim of his conducting jubilee, Henry's mind often turned back to his youth, the crowding memories that all his life were among his most cherished possessions. His parents gave him a gentle, though firm, upbringing which taught him much that was, through a topsy-turvy existence, on occasion to hold him steadily sincere and self-disciplined. His mother's singing him to sleep was a memory at which, however much he tried, he could not stop a furtive tear from falling down his cheek. His father's 'cello-playing was not only a memory of childhood, but also of his growing boyhood years—a tangible memory of encouragement coupled with a sound musical knowledge and an intense and sensitive ear for quality of tone. Above all, his father's adoration for the organ gave the boy Henry a very early love for that instrument, for he was taken anywhere and everywhere to hear good organ-playing.

When he was only seven years old, it was his parents' custom to take him every Sunday to the church of St. Sepulchre, Holborn Viaduct, where his father sang in the choir. The small boy used frequently to walk to church from their home in Oxford Street and back, holding his mother's hand and following his father, who walked ahead with Margaret Hoare, a soprano singer who was to do well later on in oratorio, and other colleagues of St. Sepulchre's choir. It was a very long walk for a small boy, but on these journeys he learned many poems and very often was given lessons in spelling by his mother.

Henry was born on 3 March 1869 at 318 Oxford Street, a few doors west of Regent Street and on the south side in the Borough of Westminster. The old house is now numbered 269. His parents were Henry Joseph Wood, son of Thomas Wood, a silversmith, and Martha Morris, daughter of Evan Morris, a farmer. They were married on 16 September 1865 at St. James's Church, Dover. In 1872 the family moved to 7 Pond Street, Hampstead, on account of their baby's health. Here they remained until 1875, when they returned to Oxford Street, moving into No. 355—now renumbered 185—where for the first time Henry Wood senior became a householder, as can be seen from the City of Westminster's books. He occupied the whole of the premises, including the shop where he carried on his occupation as optician, silversmith and model engine builder. There was a small cottage at the back of the house, which was also part of the Wood ménage.

Young Henry remained here with his parents until 3 March 1894, by when he had so far prospered in his musical career that he undertook the care of his parents and moved them to his newly acquired home at 1 Langham Place, a few doors from Queen's Hall.

When young Henry was born, father Wood occupied half a shop at 413A Oxford Street, now No. 57, where no residential accommodation was available. As the flat where young Henry was born was above a public house, Henry's birth was registered by his father as from his business address. This was to meet his wife's scruples, for Mama disliked drink in any shape or form and felt it shocking to have to live for the time being above licensed premises.

In telling of his early memories—and how often when he was most relaxed would his mind return to those days!—Henry seemed to look back wistfully to the memory of that kind safety and guidance as something lost, something for which he sought over many years.

Those years in Oxford Street and Hampstead which had moulded him had been filled with love; but, let it be remembered, love with no nonsense, for truth and sincerity in all things underlay the picture he drew so often of that home of loving and intelligent care, gradually leading him to cherish the arts of painting and music. Withal, I have often wondered whether Henry's upbringing, which had been directed with purpose in self-confidence, diligence, reliability, kindness and initiative and in which the arts of painting and music superseded even a solid continued education, after all wholly fitted him for the world which he was to face in man's estate; throughout his long career human nature and business acumen and all the hundred and one facets of life caused him one long series of shocks and surprises, disappointments and even sorrow. He was often bruised in his encounters with his fellow men because he trusted everybody.

His whole outlook centred in music and painting. He studied these arts and came to definite conclusions as to how and why he should do this or that. Then he eluded any possible self-criticism by sheer concentration until such time as he decided, through success or failure, to modify or even drastically revise an earlier decision. Having followed Henry's mind over many years, I am sure that his parents, kind, loving souls as they were, had in the progress of their son's artistic education failed to prepare him for the hazards of human nature.

In their trust and solicitude, it was always "Yes, my boy, if you wish it" when Henry sought anything from them. But the young Henry appeared to have no wishes to express outside the realms of painting and music and so wherever anything affording artistic instruction occurred in Europe or even America, the young Henry 'wished' and was sent thither, travelling by himself with written instruction, to hear the great ones of music; all at the expense of issues remotely connected with business and social contacts. Such matters remained unknown alleys into which this young boy never even peeped, his mind, right up to manhood, being bent entirely on the arts. Painting ran parallel with music, and wherever he went he never failed to see the great art galleries. In fact, he often quoted a picture as having given him inspiration which he could apply to music.

This lack of parental guidance in such matters was curious, especially in a parent so well versed in business methods as was Henry's loved father. That Henry was allowed to grow up without knowledge of the hard facts of life, of the value of money, with no mistrust or doubt, is a wonderful tribute to his parents' love and their trust in him, but his complete lack of such knowledge resulted later in an inability to watch over his own interests and found him throughout life an easy prey.

Even when a great crisis overtook him in later years, he was mystified and shocked that his unconcerned trust had been violated. In fact, until a solicitor proved it beyond doubt, he refused to believe that he had lost from his personal control capital representing more than half his savings. Guile in any shape was unknown to Henry and his upbringing left him unprotected and vulnerable.

It was not until quite late in life that this revelation of lost capital stimulated his interest in his own finances, and after the first shock of it he began to visit his bank manager and attached to himself a personal chartered accountant to look after his affairs—not only to see to money matters, but, at his special request, to meet him frequently and explain the whys and wherefores of investments, interest and the mysterious world of business matters.

Sometimes long journeys by road and other necessities ran into longish expense accounts and, as he grew accustomed to considering all this, he would call on his bank manager to make quite sure he could afford it. In fact, as in all else, once Henry had set himself to learn, his interest never waned.

Some years later he proved that he had become more alert to the business end of things. A letter arrived from an important musical organization, which, though couched in charming terms, could be read in more than one sense. He immediately spotted that the letter was ambiguous and might later lead to misunderstanding. As he did so, he remarked that it was very evident he should have had a course of business training in his youth instead of giving his whole thought to music and painting.

At the age of ten Henry had become an accomplished musician, painter and organist, as well as being a fairly proficient viola and violin player and a fine and sensitive pianist. He had studied the organ at St. Sepulchre's, and was appointed assistant organist at that church and at St. Mary's, Aldermanbury. Quite apart from his early musical development, his aptitude for painting in oils was most unusual in one so young. A small canvas painted at this early age hangs as a treasured possession in our home. 'Three Apples' is a still life of beautifully formed, ripe fruit. On the back of this canvas is still visible a note: "If ever you want to sell this little picture, Henry Wood, I will give you ten pounds for it. Ernest Nesfield." Mr. Nesfield was an architect friend of Henry Wood senior. There are some fifty pictures in my home now, and some I have given away to true friends of music since

Henry died. They date from 'Three Apples' (1880) to his last finished sketch, 'Welsh hills at low tide on the estuary from Beaumaris' (1943).

Henry was always proud of his paintings and loathed to give them away. Nevertheless some have been given to a few people who will reverence his work and memory. For instance, since Henry's death I have given one to Major Tufton Beamish, M.C., M.P. for Lewes, remembering how, when the Promenade Concerts Jubilee Fund was opened by Lord Horder and his committee in 1943, Major Beamish asked Henry if he could be of any assistance in helping the fund.

Henry was much moved by Major Beamish's approach, and more so when he knew that Major Beamish's young subaltern brother had been one of the first subscribers to the fund, giving more than he could well afford in his gratitude to Henry Wood's mission for having brought music to him and all the young people of two decades.

Major Beamish has retained his early interest and the pages of Hansard bear witness to the way in which his questions in the House have centred interest in what is now the Henry Wood National Memorial. The form of the memorial is now agreed by the government, and a hall to provide rehearsals for a full symphony orchestra and a choir of 300 is to be built within the site of the old Queen's Hall. It will be called the 'Henry Wood Rehearsal Hall' or a similar name. Major Beamish's interest all these years has been retained by the memory of his young brother, who died on war service soon after he had made his contribution of fifty pounds, coupled with his regard for Henry's music.

Henry's canvases still lay almost entirely in the future, however, when at the age of eleven he decided to become a musician. The decision was not made, he often related, until he

had weighed the problem of earning his living and decided
that painting held very little prospect for a mere youngster
with no money behind him. Early in 1881 he made his first
public appearance as a musician. He appeared as accompanist
at a concert given at Corpus Christi Church, Maiden Lane,
arranged for the benefit of the school incorporated in the
church. At this concert, the twelve-year-old boy accompanied
songs sung by Agnes Larcom and Madame Osborne Williams,
two artists who were to be well known in the world of singing, and also took part in string quartets in which his father
was the 'cellist.

A short time ago, quite by chance, I received a vivid account
of Henry's life at this time. I was buying some film for my
camera, and began discussing the taking of photographs—an
art in which I am fairly proficient—with the owner of the
shop in Wigmore Street. One thing led to another and I discovered that this quiet, elderly man's name was Bannister.
"Not *Dr.* Bannister's son?" I inquired. "Yes," he said. "Then
do tell me all you know," I begged, "because you were a
playmate of Henry's young days."

And Mr. Bannister recounted his memories of the Wood
home as the young Henry learnt to love and understand
music.

"My early recollections of Sir Henry Wood," he told me,
"go back a long way. I knew him as 'Joey', the name his
parents always called him since his father's name was also
Henry. I was born in 1868, so was about the same age as
'Joey'. My father, Dr. Bannister, was an old friend of the
Woods, and as he lived at 436 Oxford Street they were
neighbours.

"In those days there were no large shops, and in most cases

the proprietors lived over their businesses. I often went to tea at the Woods', and after tea Joey and I went into the back basement which was used as a workshop, where there were two men who made large model locomotives and engines. They were very proud of their work and fond of showing us boys how they made the engines.

"This basement, being paved with stone slabs, was very useful for us to set the engines going. After Mr. Wood had closed the shop we all went to the drawing-room on the first floor, and Mr. Wood practised on the 'cello, Mrs. Wood on the piano and Joey on the violin. I am sure they were all very good musicians and enjoyed it—more than I did, I am afraid, for being only about ten or eleven years old I may have been a little bored, especially as in those days the only illumination was a single gas burner and the room was almost in darkness.

"I have a very vivid recollection of having to sit on a cold horsehair chair, which was not very comfortable as the horse-hairs stuck in my legs.

"I was quite a different sort of boy from Joey; for one thing he was very fond of music and would play the same portion over and over until he was perfect; other favourite pursuits were drawing and painting. These did not interest me as much as playing cricket or playing with the engines.

"When Joey played the organ at St. Sepulchre's Church, we used to walk there on Friday evenings for practice and also on Sundays. Mr. and Mrs. Wood went by omnibus, which cost 4*d.* Soon afterwards, my parents moved to Russell Square and we lost touch with one another."

In 1883 the young organist was engaged to give nine organ recitals at the Fisheries Exhibition at the Royal Albert Hall. A specimen programme gives an idea of his spirit of adventure and musicianly thought in programme-making, and also

of its length which must have entailed an exacting performance in the unusually short-legged little boy. It was necessary,
he told me, "literally to stand on the pedals":

Great Dragon 'Samson'	*Handel*
Minuet and Trio	*Haydn*
Gavotte	*Rameau*
The Lullaby	*Stace*
Marcia Religioso	*Gluck*
Trio, Andante and Rondo	*Haydn*
Minuet 'Samson'	*Handel*
Pastoral Prelude	*Gordigiani*
March 'Judas Maccabeus'	*Handel*
Movement, arranged from a Sonata	*Beethoven*
Wedding March	*Mendelssohn*

From this time Henry was working almost without a break,
accompanying at concerts and taking choral rehearsals not
only at the churches where he was acting as organist but anywhere and everywhere, to give him an opportunity to learn.
It is difficult to connect these youthful years with any very
definite schooling, for although he was a pupil at a school in
Argyll Street, Oxford Street, it seems to have been a sketchy
education; he used to say how tired he would be when breakfast called him at 7.30 a.m. before leaving for school. It was
an early start for a lad who may have spent a tiring night at
a concert or recital.

In 1885 he was engaged to give a series of organ recitals at
the International Fisheries Exhibition at South Kensington on
the Wedlake organ, with programmes of extensive length and
varied interest. A sample programme gives us an idea of how
his work had expanded by the time he was sixteen:

Hertoise in D minor	*Lott*
Overture 'Athalie'	*Mendelssohn*
My heart ever faithful	*J. S. Bach*
Fugue after Bach	*Schumann*
Larghetto (Clarinet Quintet, Op. 108)	*Mozart*
Offertoire	*Capocci*
Prelude and Fugue in G	*J. S. Bach*
Second Concerto	*J. S. Bach*
By the Waters	*Handel*

I read an article a short time ago in *Musical Opinion* in which the writer, Frances T. Kennard, called attention to Henry's "marvellous acumen for accurate details at the tender age of fifteen in the use of Bach's initials when it was not customary" and reflected that it was this meticulous attention to detail which not only made the early days of the Promenade Concerts possible, but was evident throughout his public and private life. It was indeed an attribute rarely met with, especially when we note the unpreparedness with which some musicians approach a rehearsal in these days.

With Henry, self-discipline was an inborn attribute which nothing could disarrange or distort. Its value can be fully appreciated by those who worked with him not only through the years, but especially in the early days when, in 1895, the Queen's Hall Orchestra was formed and the Proms were born. Six Promenade Concerts a week with only three rehearsals for all six, throughout a ten-weeks' season, and along with this gigantic task the Saturday and Sunday afternoon symphony concerts at Queen's Hall—sometimes two in a day: that was the weight he had to carry then. If self-discipline had not been Henry's outstanding trait, it is surely doubtful whether the

Proms would have survived five years, let alone fifty during his life—and under his sole direction throughout.

In 1886 Henry was engaged for a series of organ recitals at the Art Treasures Exhibition at Folkestone. There were two programmes a day. In September 1886 Henry's name appears in programmes as a composer, and we find solo pianist Mr. Henry J. Wood accompanying his Op. 2, Romance in C for Violin and Piano.

At the age of seventeen he began teaching singing at 185 Oxford Street, gathering together a connection all too numerous to allow himself the time he needed for composition. In his later years, when he was constantly reviewing some of the wide artistic interests which absorbed him, he felt that he should have continued composition. He began composing before he was ten. In 1888 the Press acclaimed him a composer of distinction when two of his songs were sung at a Royal Academy concert, and received more than usual attention. "Two really charming songs composed by Henry J. Wood were 'The Sea hath its Pearls' and 'When on my Couch I'm lying'. The verses are by Heine, the German poet. 'The Sea hath its Pearls' is quite a gem and reflected great credit on the composer," a writer declared in *Era* on 24 March 1888.

After 1886 some twenty-seven songs were published in the space of two years, and in 1889 his comic opera *Zuleika*, the oratorio *St. Dorothea* and a sacred cantata *Joseph* were produced. The year 1890 saw the comedy opera *Daisy*, comic operetta *Returning the Compliment*, a cantata *Nacoochee* founded on an Indian legend, and *A Butterfly Queen*. The pastoral operetta *A Hundred Years Ago* was produced and ran a long time at the Royalty Theatre, London, in 1893. In 1894 he composed a really lovely scene, *Jacob's Lament*, and anthems,

Acts II, 2-4, and St. John XIV, 15, 16, 18 and 21. Much chamber music took shape, and his songs were sung by such well-known artists of the period as Marie Roze and Ben Davies, among others.

In addition to his composing, Henry was organist in succession at St. Sepulchre's, St. Mary's, Aldermanbury and St. John's, Fulham; in 1891 he conducted the Carl Rosa company for the Marie Roze seasons of *Carmen*, and in 1892 produced at the Royalty Theatre, London, Tchaikovsky's opera *Eugene Onegin* alternately with his direction of *Maritana* during Signor Lago's opera season. It is curious to note that then, as now, argument reigned regarding foreign artists. One London paper said of *Eugene Onegin* that as well as "such artists as Charles Manners, Fanny Moody, the orchestra, be it remarked too, was under the direction of another Englishman, Mr. Henry J. Wood. The British public have, it will be seen, reason to thank Signor Lago for his very liberal support of native talent."

The paper added: "Tchaikovsky's opera was thoroughly successful and on the fall of the curtain the principal singers, Signor Lago (who sponsored the season) and Mr. Wood, the excellent conductor, were called for and applauded with enthusiasm."

Another item of Press comment on the same performance said the orchestra "under the able conductorship of Henry J. Wood exemplified a spartan discipline with the nicest time and perfection both in stringed and wind instrument, in every way satisfactory." And, remember, at this time Henry Wood was twenty-three years old!

On top of all these activities there was his work as a professor of singing. But teaching the 'gentle art' remained always a form of recreation. He loved the human voice, and in many cases gave of his knowledge in this field without fee of any kind to a promising voice. The methods he advocated then have been recorded in his monumental work *The Gentle Art of Singing*. Here is the timetable he set for singing-students. It is quoted (by kind permission of the O.U.P.) from the Appendix, Vol. 1:

"So many students of singing have no idea of planning their day's work. The singing-student cannot, like the pianist, sit down for a solid three or four hours' grind at a stretch, but must apportion his work carefully in order not to fatigue his voice. Once the freshness and bloom are off a voice, it almost never recovers. Only in a few instances has a tired singing voice been restored by long silence. The following is a rough sketch of how a student might plan out his time:

"*Daily before breakfast.* Half an hour's physical exercises. Muller's exercises are quite good, and he has published a book for men and women.

"*8.30 to 9 a.m. After Breakfast.* Walk in all weathers. Paper work. At first this will consist of the elements of music, elements of harmony, etc., and later harmony and counterpoint.

"*9 to 10 a.m.* Transposing your songs, arias and exercises. Writing out the words of all your songs and arias by the various authors, not as set by the composers with repetitions, etc. Making your own literal translations of all foreign songs and arias.

"*10 a.m.* 10 minutes' breathing exercises for singing without voice.

"*10.10 a.m.* Vocal exercises (after one year this can be extended from ten to fifteen minutes).

SIR HENRY WOOD IN 1939

RACHMANINOFF AND SIR HENRY. JUBILEE CONCERT, 1938

"*10.20 a.m.* Rest voice.

"*10.30 a.m.* Work mentally at your vocal exercises; do not hum or sing, but you can play them through many, many times on the piano, always slowly and in perfect rhythm.

"*10.50 a.m.* Vocal exercises (after one year these can be increased to fifteen minutes).

"*11 a.m.* Rest.

"*11.15 to 12.* Practise the pianoforte.

"*12 noon.* Ear-training exercises. Interval-training exercises. If you can possibly arrange for another singing-student to join you for this hour every day it will be of the utmost benefit to you both, as he can play all the ear-training exercises, and the musical interval dictation exercises for you, and you can do the same for him. And no harm would be done to your voices if you sang Greenwood's (published by Novello) two-part exercises—without any pianoforte prop—for the final ten minutes, quietly and calmly as reading practice.

"*1-3 p.m.* Rest. Walk for an hour. Memorize words and notes for to-morrow's work. Study languages, also works on phonology, phonetics and read all standard poetical works.

"*4 p.m.* Vocal exercises. After two years' study, these can be extended to nearly an hour—of course with plenty of rests, and to work with your accompanist. (Classical *lieder*, fine English songs, arias, operas, and oratorios.)

"*4.15 p.m.* Read and study musical history and works on various musical subjects, of which a very fine educational series is now published. Read the lives of great composers and the plots of operas.

"*5 p.m.* Rest.

"*6-7 p.m.* Practise the pianoforte, and look over the words and music of any work you may be going to hear this week.

"*8 p.m.* On three nights a week, if possible, attend the performance of an opera, an oratorio, a chamber music concert or a vocal recital.

"Never let a week pass without attending a string quartet or chamber concert. Your ear will thus be attuned to just intonation; you will hear music of the first order and you will become accustomed to hearing and following four parts. Buy from time to time miniature scores of the classical quartets; study them, at first stave by stave, and then two staves at a time, and as soon as you are able all four parts (from the 'cello upwards). This is one of the most important acts of your musical education. You cannot get the full benefit of your visits to concert and opera unless you work really hard studying words and music of all you go to hear. A Wagner opera you may study for five years before you begin to know anything about it—at least this is my experience of many students. When you go to hear *The Ring*, think what a vast enterprise it is really to enter into the spirit of this colossal masterpiece, and so on. *In bed* every night at 10 p.m. when not out at a musical performance."

Even Sunday is set to some rule, of which extracts show how Henry Wood instructed his pupils, and how he regarded the essential element in the gradual training of the singing voice and general musicianship:

"*Sunday morning.* If you live in a cathedral city or in London, attend different services every Sunday, when you will hear the dignified schools of church music, etc. Sunday afternoons, if living in London, attend a classical orchestral concert. After a time you should be able to call up in your mind's ear the sound of three flutes, two clarinets, two bassoons, the sound of four horns, the sound of trumpets and trombones, of drums and percussion instruments, and the harp. This will help you tremendously later on when you sing with an orchestra for the first time. Sunday evenings you may visit your friends and receive your friends, provided your work for the coming week is ready. Do not dance in stuffy, crowded dance-halls; all singers require all the fresh air possible; walk in preference in any weather out in the open air. Visit picture galleries whenever possible; pictures are a help to visual memory and help to create imagination. Keep a small piano in your bedroom, never practise in a room where people are in and out to distract."

From the age of ten Henry started to save his pocket-money in order to purchase all the music he required. In many organ works now in the Music Library which Sir Henry gave to the Royal Academy of Music to commemorate his fifty years as a professional conductor can be seen the markings of this youthful musician.

Henry followed this method all his life, and accumulated as the years went by a musician's personal library unlikely to be duplicated anywhere. This library, by means of which he always had at hand works bearing his personal markings, enabled him to tackle those early days of his Queen's Hall Orchestra and the first years of the Queen's Hall Promenade Concerts when Robert Newman, astute manager as he was, was interested more in cramming in the maximum number of concerts a week than faultless presentation. Henry's personal library afforded him time for careful study and advance preparation for rehearsals and enabled him to achieve orchestral finesse which has not been surpassed even in these days.

Henry used to be very amused when he heard how his blue-pencil markings were a cause of derision among certain people who, in later days—from 1938 onwards—were fortunate enough to have managements who provided adequate rehearsal, largely as a result of Henry Wood's building of a music-conscious public.

One writer on music even went to the trouble of decrying Henry's blue-pencil markings in Beethoven scores. How little could this writer have known of Henry Wood's early pioneer work for music, and his latter-day presentation! It is undeniable by even the most reluctant to give credit where credit is due that Henry Wood's pioneer work, year in and year out, teaching a young public through his Queen's Hall Orchestra, resulted in the large music-loving public we have to-day and the wide platform open to receive all young conductors, young artists and young composers, provided they are real musicians. Henry's blue-pencil markings always reveal sensitive musicianship and regard for the composer—and anyone who takes advantage of the Sir Henry Wood Library which Henry gave to the R.A.M., now housed at the Royal Academy, can see and learn much of the wisdom evinced and the keen knowledge of the instruments of the orchestra and the score. The works of the library can be hired for a small fee which goes to the Henry Wood Fund to assist necessitous students. The fund helps the young student who is in need of a new frock, a suit, string, or in fact anything which will assist at a first appearance during student days. Henry instituted this fund because he had often seen a student of particular ability become self-conscious at a students' public concert in the Duke's Hall, or in Queen's Hall, because of a poor pair of shoes or the need of a new bow or strings.

Do not run away with the idea that one of young Henry

Wood's blue-pencil markings remained a fixed direction every time he conducted that particular work. His preparation for each rehearsal or concert was always as if a new score were placed before him. Through the years his readings varied considerably, although his blue-pencil reminders to give so-and-so a careful direction, that here an oboe lead is too covered, there to keep the strings down, etc., still apply and are immensely useful for a young would-be conductor to study. How about those blue markings which remain in the parts? Well, the answer is that no professional player ever misunderstood Henry's stick, and no member of the orchestra ever escaped his eye, his direction and unmistakable 'request'.

I know only too well what silly jokes and wisecracks are exchanged among a certain set of musicians on this 'blue pencil' of Henry, but I often wonder if they know that young Henry Wood was the first to institute bow-marks in orchestral parts, and if they comprehend the untold artistic value of Henry's disciplinary markings in relation to orchestral playing to-day? Do they realize that Henry's bowings in those days way back have been the means of producing orchestra string tone, quality and phrasing as we know it—and insist upon—to-day? Do they know that at that period, in the old St. James's Hall concerts under Richter and Augustus Manns, the players bowed as they pleased, some up, some down, and it took young Henry Wood to see and note what could be done for greater artistic results and to have the courage to impose his blue-pencil discipline?

Henry often spoke of the derision with which the old go-as-you-please orchestral player of those days scanned the orchestral parts he prepared—and some players can still be found able to make fun of the blue pencil, apparently unaware that they owe to Henry Wood the institution of what is now a worldwide custom—indeed, a *sine qua non* of orchestral playing everywhere.

In those early years, Henry loved the old Queen's Hall Saturday afternoon symphony concerts, for here he was given adequate rehearsal. When I say adequate, I mean that the programme required more than Robert Newman's usual one rehearsal—or one rehearsal for two concerts. For the Saturday afternoon concerts Henry could get a second rehearsal. With even this very small margin he was able to give much which was of the highest order, and so gathered round him a public intent upon learning and also upon stern criticism. In later years I became acutely aware that Henry was conscious of one undeniable fact, that in his early pioneer work for music—to bring the great classical repertoire to the man in the street through his Promenade Concerts—he had ruthlessly thrust aside his longing for that artistic perfection which a less exacting dedication to his fellow men would have secured him. He had had no time of his own, year in and year out.

I found unmistakable realization of this in later years, and it is generally agreed that this was so after studying his profound readings of Brahms and Haydn and noting his deep insight into the works of Elgar—above all *The Dream of Gerontius*; but the symphonies, too, were peculiarly revealing under Henry's direction. "Ah, my dear," he so often said, "I have never had all the time I needed, entirely my own! It has been so difficult. What time I had for myself I gave to the study of Bach—*dear John Sebastian Bach*."

He always said this in that caressing voice, just as he would ask me in times of stress or extreme tiredness:

"Read me, dear Jessie, some Anna Magdalena Bach."

Henry did not restrict his horizon by concentrating on a favourite composer, however. To him every line of music was

70

there to be read into and to be rendered with every ounce of musicianship within him. I have seen him examine a new manuscript, turn the pages and exclaim:

"Oh, my! This is a dreadful work!"

Yet at rehearsal and performance no one could think otherwise than that this 'first performance' was a work of his own particular choice. Heart and soul were given to his musicianly direction of the orchestra.

Mrs. Rosa Newmarch, writing on the occasion of his fortieth Promenade season, said (*The Chesterian*, 1934):

"Henry Wood once said to me many years ago that it was his ambition to become a great *professional* conductor, by which I understood him to mean a conductor who builds his reputation on a large comprehensive conception of the Art, not merely on a certain knack with one special branch of music or one individual composer; a man who chooses his work when possible, but does his level best with whatever may chance to go against the grain; who may sigh for the unattainably perfect orchestra, but who spares himself no pains to put a fine edge on any tools that come his way. Looking back over his lengthening career, there is no denying that Henry Wood has achieved his ambition to deal faithfully with all kinds of music and musicians."

That was the road young Mr. Wood stepped out upon that night of 10 August 1895, when he conducted the first Promenade Concert. It was, we now know, a red-letter day for Henry Wood, for coming musicians and public alike. His parents were present, standing among the promenaders almost under the rostrum, according to that never-to-be-forgotten singer, Agnes Nicholls (later Lady Harty), who stood beside them. She was then a young student. One well-known soprano who made her appearance in 1893 is still a devotee of the Promenade Concerts. She is Winifred Ludlam. She, too, was in the Queen's Hall that night, and she remembers the calm contented joy of both parents as they stood and saw their son acclaimed on the road to which they had steered him so successfully.

Henry himself often spoke of that day as their great day; and he would mention their pride to see him on the rostrum, then add:

"Mother died very soon afterwards. I was thankful she saw the start of the Proms."

CHAPTER 4

Into War

HENRY SEEMED VERY tired in the early part of 1939, and it was apparent that the strain of making speeches and attending functions in connection with his conducting jubilee had taken its toll. He always hated public speaking. "Please do not book anything of the kind for me," he had asked, and I had carried out his request—as always—as far as I could. But so much had been involved in the jubilee, so many musical organizations had wished to pay him tribute, that some speech-making had been unavoidable—even if it might sometimes be limited to a few words of thanks.

When speaking in public he was nervous, although there was no visible sign of his discomfort. Only those who knew his every expression would note the involuntary closing of the eyelid, the little twitch of the left cheek—the outcome of a facial paralysis when he was twelve years old, brought on by too diligent study. The nervous tensions while he was speaking could even be detected by a slight yellow suffusion of the rim of his ear. "I've learnt to speak with my baton, and any other way is a worry," he told me. But speeches were terribly difficult to avoid. All those appreciative people, generous in their tributes, expected a personal reply. That was the pity, for I knew and worried about the restless night and fatigue of the day following each such occasion.

Thank goodness, early 1939 did not find Henry overloaded with work, and he devoted his free days to teaching his beloved art of singing. He was never so happy as at the piano listening

73

and watching singers, helping them to acquire sound principles in their art. He gave confidence and—in public—assurance that he could be counted on to accompany them not only faithfully, but with a silent sympathy of understanding to carry them through when sometimes courage failed. His benign look down from the rostrum conveyed his reverence for the singer and assisted any faltering through difficult passages or, as sometimes happened, a sudden attack of 'nerves'.

All the usual festivals up and down the country found Henry a gay and good colleague. Scarborough—how he liked dear Kneale Kelly, the conductor of the very good little orchestra there; and Eastbourne, where poor Captain Ames, then nearly blind, was wonderfully brave and always debonair. He wrote Henry a letter from Wiesbaden which shows his cheerful courage:

"Dear Sir Henry,

"I am so glad to see that you are coming here next week. Is there anything I can do for you? Have you got your rooms, etc.? I ask this as the hotels are booking up quickly now that the season has commenced.

"I came here to see and consult Professor Pagenstecker, and he put me at once into the Klinik, as my case is so very serious. I'm quickly going blind through a tumour pressing on the optic nerve and killing it. I'm sorry to say it is too late to save the left eye, as it is too far gone, but he is trying to save what is left of the right. I have half-vision in that, but can only read one word at a time.

"It makes me so mad when I think of the time I wasted in a London nursing home three months ago—all to no purpose.

"However, that is my trouble.

74

"Please don't hesitate to let me do something if I can be of use. It will be a relief to have something to do. At any rate I hope you will let me see you when you come,

"Sincerely,

"H. G. Ames."

I wonder, is it a worse affliction to be deaf?

Dame Ethel Smyth, who had become deaf, told us that nothing remained in life without the sound of birds and dogs, of trees rustling in the wind, without the sound of the sea. It was the loss of these things which left her with a sense of aloneness, for music had always been a silent picture from brain to paper for her which needed no articulate sound. "Although," she hastened to add, "it was jolly nice to hear one's stuff whenever anyone had the kindness to play it." In those words Henry sensed the gratitude she had for his repeated remembrances.

The Proms of 1939 started with the depressing, disheartening crisis in the air that gripped a civilization slithering rapidly into a second world war. But at Queen's Hall there was the daily delight of music-making with a great orchestra. Defying the gloom in the atmosphere, the B.B.C. orchestra never played better. But it was not to be. On Friday 1 September there was a Beethoven night which included the *Pastoral Symphony*, Harriet Cohen in the Piano Concerto No. 2 in B flat, and John Fullard singing the song cycle *An die ferne Geliebte*. Fullard, a young recent student of the Royal Academy of Music, gave Henry much hope for a splendid future on this his first appearance at a Promenade Concert. "A Dance Poem" was to have been given its first performance directed by the composer—Frank Bridge—but, alas, to a rapt and packed Queen's Hall came direction from the B.B.C., immediately after the performance

of the symphony, that we end the concert forthwith. Ever
since the Nazi invasion of Poland earlier in the day war had
seemed inevitable, and, although Henry was well aware of the
fact, he still cherished the hope that the concerts would proceed, come what may, as in 1914, when Queen's Hall, under
the management of Robert Newman, refused to put up the
shutters. Memories of his mission throughout the first world
war, when he and his Queen's Hall Orchestra played on,
sharpened Henry's shocked sorrow when the B.B.C. thus
closed the season. He concealed his emotion and went on to
the platform to bid good night to the orchestra and members
of the public. Quite simply he said: "My dear friends I thank
you for your loyal support and I hope we shall soon meet
again."

After that he uttered no word. He ate no supper. There
was just numb sorrow that night for him.

We drove home in darkness—a blackout we were to endure
for many years had already descended on London. Henry
never again saw a street fully lit—he died before the end of
the war.

The B.B.C. departed, we knew not where; there was no
word—and no indication as to the rest of the season.

All Henry's musical activities were now centred on his firm
determination to remain, as in the first world war, in London
or very near to it, and to do all in his power to assist his fellow
musicians.

At this time he was to have received an honorary degree
from the University of London with the usual academic ritual
but owing to war the ceremony had to be cancelled and the
scroll was sent to him by messenger. This tribute from his
own London gave him a very comforting pleasure, indeed a
thrill of gratitude, though he had been similarly honoured by

Cambridge, Oxford, Manchester and Birmingham, as well as France and Belgium.

One affectionate memory of the early days of the war was his direction of a section of Boyd Neel's orchestra at the National Gallery on 23 November, soon after Dame Myra Hess had started the series of lunch-time concerts. Henry loved those strings that day, and he deeply respected the splendid efforts of Dame Myra, backed so enthusiastically by Sir Kenneth Clark, then Director of the National Gallery. Not only did the concerts encourage and comfort all those bound by their duties to remain in London but they employed many young artists who, owing to the war, might have lost their valuable years of training. Further, they gave to established artists the privilege of sending the message of support which music was able to give the workers of our sorely-tried city.

With the London Symphony Orchestra and the London Philharmonic Orchestra, Henry began a succession of journeys to the theatres of greater London and the home counties. Rain or fine, hail or snow, bombs or bangs always found Henry willing to turn out once he had adjusted himself to the misery of blackout conditions. Happily for his health he could stand any amount of heat, for these theatres and halls seemed to have no ventilation. The heat and lack of air often became almost unbearable, horribly so on a wet night. But the spiritual relaxation enjoyed by those huge audiences was obvious.

George Wood, then the manager of the L.S.O., was wonderfully kind and looked after us with that forethought and care one associates with the impresario in the great, good old days of Patti, Melba and such stars, unusual in latter days. George Wood, however, had been an orchestral musician in the Queen's Hall Orchestra and really loved old values—and, incidentally, 'Timber'.

I always tried to take food with me when we travelled, as only in that way was I sure that Henry ate something good, not the dreadful stuff, concocted anyhow, to which so many had become subjected for want of enterprise and care on the part of restaurateurs and hotel managements. If only every hotel would engage a chef competent to cook and serve fresh vegetables of good colour and consistency, they would not only attract and retain their custom but save large sums on meat, poultry, game, etc. Poor old potato! Even new ones would turn up soft and spongy, and as for that slimy mess masquerading as 'mashed potato', it was only fit for paste for paper-hanging!

The stress and anxiety caused at this time over the future of the Promenade Concerts left Henry limp, cross and fidgety. There were endless talks with the B.B.C. music department which led nowhere. While Henry's anxiety was for music, my anxiety was for his health far more.

I look back and blame myself for lack of courage and initiative in failing to take the matter up on Henry's behalf on the highest level. I was to learn a few years later the wisdom of approaching the highest quarters direct. It was necessary, not because of any want of knowledge or kindness, musical and political, in the music department personnel, who were always staunch in their work for and with Henry, but not only did the system of civil service routine take up immeasurable time, the maze of correspondence from one person to another was such that the point was often lost and some specific issue would eventually reach the fountain-head with or without Henry's expressed wishes and decisions, or return to Henry without a precise decision.

On this occasion, however, I did not attempt any short cut. Whatever the result of such an approach might have been, it would have saved Henry much needless fret, an anxiety not personal but for music, musicians and young music lovers.

There was a plethora of would-be sponsors for a 1940 Promenade season, but the arrangements and negotiations became entangled in a skein of complications and misunderstandings that Henry felt need never have occurred. Amid these troubles, nothing seemed right for Henry, however one tried: to console was to run the risk of being considered wanting in foresight and sympathy; to advise a wait-and-see policy gave Henry a feeling of frustration which took every ounce of initiative from him and left only a leaden indifference which, once it had taken hold, required patience and ingenuity to disperse. We spent Christmas in Sussex, but in spite of my hope that a few days' respite away from the immediate scene would relieve the stress under which he seethed, it only entrenched him further into cold despondency. Inaction was something quite unfamiliar to Henry, and although the B.B.C. had taken over responsibility for the Promenade Concerts thirteen years ago when in 1926 Robert Newman died, Henry could not accustom himself to methods of less speedy action. In Henry's autobiography he says of Robert Newman: "I cannot express here all I felt at dear Robert Newman's passing. For thirty-one years we had worked side by side; we had been such firm friends. Our friendship had been built and maintained on an artistic and business basis, even though neither of our private lives seemed to enter into it. We never argued and we never fell out.... We discussed every detail from all angles calmly and in the kindliest spirit. In his dealings with me he was as straight as a die and always enthusiastic. I feel I shall never look upon his like again." After three decades with Robert Newman, it is not to be wondered at that Henry chafed at delays. It was a sorry time for Henry, and would have been even more distressing had he known of the prevailing feeling at Broadcasting House (which we learned afterwards) that there was no copyright in the title of the Promenade Concerts in spite of the fact, clear to all, that Henry Wood *was* Promenade Concerts. However, the feeling among some at the B.B.C. was that if Queen's Hall started on a Promenade season independently of the B.B.C., the B.B.C. could run their own Promenade Concerts in opposition elsewhere.

On looking back it is a very simple matter to see how such an *impasse* could have been avoided, but the destruction of Henry's trust left him bitter and quickly irritated and less amenable when reviewing a forward musical calendar.

It must be remembered that Mr. Owen Mase had represented the B.B.C. music department for many years, and that he had been 'granted leave' by the B.B.C. to carry out arrangements for the London Festival in 1939, which the B.B.C. had practically sponsored and which, of course, embraced the Toscanini concerts. It now looked to Henry as if this sort of 'leave' was one which the B.B.C. considered more generally advisable in their own interests. All this made Henry feel quite sure that Mr. Mase was still a B.B.C. employee, acting *sub rosa*, when in December 1939 and January 1940 he approached Henry regarding the 1940 season of Promenade Concerts at Queen's Hall. Henry was firmly of the opinion that, for some domestic or political reason, the corporation could not during wartime enter the open field of concert-giving but wished to arrange things in this manner.

Thus Henry thought he was assisting the corporation to adjust itself to a policy forced upon it through the exigencies of war as he cautiously continued talks with various parties in and outside the B.B.C. This was—as one can now see—a fruitful source of misunderstandings. Weeks and months of palaver, all the miserable complicated verbal comings and goings between Bristol, where the B.B.C. Orchestra and music department had now settled down, and London could have been avoided had Henry realized in the first instance that Mr. Owen Mase was no longer a member of the staff.

Henry wrote to Mr. Mase on 8 January 1940 asking whether the B.B.C. had come to a final decision regarding the 1940 season of summer Promenade Concerts. "If so," Henry wrote, "they surely in all decency should have advised me of that decision." This letter was followed by my personal telephone conversation with Mr. Mase, advising him that Henry must know whether he had the blessing of the B.B.C. in proceeding with Mr. Mase's project to run the summer season in company with Mr. Keith Douglas. Mr. Mase wrote on 9 January confirming our telephone conversation that there was nothing to worry about and that everything was friendly with the B.B.C. "Indeed," he continued in this letter, "I would not be doing what I am to bridge difficulties on any other terms." Thus Henry felt that even though the Proms might have to be run by proxy, as it were, it was at least a gesture in the right spirit.

Meetings with Mr. Owen Mase, Mr. Dreyfus—Director of Messrs. Chappell and Co., the music publishers and lessees of Queen's Hall—Mr. Keith Douglas, Mr. Harold Holt and representatives of the B.B.C., continued from time to time until 9 February 1940, when the B.B.C. conveyed a verbal message via their concert manager, Mr. W. W. Thompson, that they would not sponsor the 1940 season.

There was no movement, not even of an eyelash, as Henry, like a stone and as cold, told Mr. Thompson:

"I cannot accept a verbal message on such a momentous matter—in fact, I have not received the message and shall require in writing what the B.B.C. have to say; not merely as it is of vital public interest, but as a matter of courtesy to myself."

The message, however, completely broke down all Henry's hopeful trust, and convinced him that no more time must be wasted if the 1940 Promenade Concerts were to mature. Henry's feelings? I find it difficult to describe his attitude; he was cold, stubborn and angry; resentment seemed to have entered his soul, and, as for lucid arguments, well, he was only grimly determined somehow to 'get on with the job'.

Henry heard nothing definite until 4 March 1940, when the B.B.C. sent him a letter from which I quote stating that arguments between themselves and Messrs. Chappell had not resulted in solving certain problems in relation to contractual arrangements for Queen's Hall. "We do not know how long the argument will continue or what it will lead to. Until it is settled you can well imagine we cannot make any decision about Promenade Concerts this summer," the letter said.

This frightening, unbelievable destruction, not only of Henry's life's work for music but of his trust, left him with a silent burning anger. That this long period of uncertainty should end in this sorry fashion broke his spirit entirely.

Following the break which the B.B.C. had made, preparations and agreement on a programme for a 1940 Promenade season at Queen's Hall went ahead. The concerts were to be sponsored by Keith Douglas and Owen Mase, with Messrs. Chappell in the background with a watching brief. The complex arrangements were happily simplified through the efforts of John Tillett, that well-known impresario of the old tradition. He was a tower of strength to Henry in this wibbly-wobbly set-up, for poor old Henry's resentment, though inarticulate—his previous serenity had given way to a forced sociability—still smouldered, ready to break forth at any moment.

Having decided on his management, it took Henry greatly by surprise when he learned that it was proposed to present the season under the banner of the Royal Philharmonic Society. Mr. Douglas, the society's honorary secretary, had for many years financed and backed the society with all his power as it ploughed its way through difficult times, so when he told Henry: "I want the royal coat-of-arms on the Promenade Concert programmes," it was so obviously an earnest desire on his part that Henry agreed, although very reluctantly. As he said, what really matters is that the Proms go on.

The 1940 season was announced as Henry's last. Keith Douglas suggested this as a stunt to bring together an audience which might be timorous of blackout and bombs, but who would perhaps venture if they thought it was to be their last chance of seeing their idol, 'Henry J.' Henry's tacit agreement was merely a dull, disinterested acquiescence, given at a time when a mood of black depression had followed the months of trial. He just did not care what they did. I argued the point with him, but to no avail. "Let them go on with what they will. I'm tired of arguments over my concerts," he exclaimed. Thus he allowed himself to emulate the prima donna of the past; but in all his long life it was his first primadonnaism—and it was never repeated.

The new management was as virgin soil on which seeds of impatience throve. They were slow to move, much less to go forward with engaging artists and making all the other urgent preparations for a major concert season. All this made Henry irritable at times, for which I was not only thankful but greatly relieved, as it drew him out of the indifference, almost despair, which came near to breaking him.

"I must move heaven and earth to get things on," now became his constant urge. Sometimes, throwing his usual kindness to the winds, he would write a curt, to-the-point letter in his big, firm hand to the new management, urging them to action. There were toiling weeks of fevered anxiety before the programmes were ready at last. Only those who knew how Henry approached the Promenade Concerts each year with the same intense sincerity could feel at that time the strain imposed on him by the delay. Another man would have given up the unequal struggle, for already he was months behind the time when, all artists engaged, programme proofs should have been ready. Yet here he was at the end of April, literally forcing his new management to get the prospectus out.

My own intimate knowledge of music, of his methods, and of his work enabled me to smooth away hundreds of problems for him. I recollect one blunder, though, which no amount of tact could make a smooth discussion. It was when the management had suggested cutting down the fees of artists and orchestra. I proposed instead that we ourselves should undertake sponsorship of the Promenade Concert. "What? Me? A manager on my own behalf? Never! Never!" Henry exclaimed. But that became nearer a fact than Henry anticipated when so many obstacles and so many departures from the traditions of the Proms were pressed upon him that he flatly refused to proceed with the season's arrangements. "All right," said Keith Douglas, "if you don't conduct, Sir Henry, then I shall." Indeed, Keith Douglas took the L.S.O. on tour when raids shut us down. After that Henry glued himself to a task which for the previous forty-four years had been a labour of love. Of course, Henry would have preferred to accept Mr. Dreyfus's suggestion to continue his Promenade Concerts under the management of Harold Holt, for he was versed in such work, and had an office and staff accustomed to dealing with artists, but Harold's first remark when Henry met him to discuss the possibility was: "I hope you'll agree, Sir Henry, to contracting the orchestras at reduced terms for such an engagement." Ah! he didn't know Henry—"Well, there's plenty of time, Mr. Holt, and I'm just rushing off to an R.A.M. rehearsal." Henry would never agree to that. It is strange how things leak out, though, for the very next day when Henry was conducting his senior orchestra at the R.A.M. a deputation from the L.P.O. waited on him urging 'usual terms'.

Gradually the buoyant step returned, however. The Proms would go on after all, and Henry refused to allow air-raids, warnings or blackout to assail his determination to keep the flag flying. During March, April and May he was occupied with concerts up and down the country as well as in London and greater London. Nothing was cancelled on account of war.

When time permitted, we stayed at our home in Hove and Henry was able to enjoy peacefully quite lovely spring weather. It was here that Henry saw Sir Hamilton Harty for the last time. He was a very ill man when he came to lunch with us one day, but was still full of enthusiasm and agreed to give Henry a new work for the 1940 Promenade Concerts. It was to be a *Chopin Suite*, but was not quite ready in time, though I believe it was very nearly completed, if not entirely, before Harty died later the same year. I wonder what became of the manuscript—it would be a work worth hearing.

The Langham Hotel again became our headquarters for the Promenade season and other London concerts. From our rooms on the third floor we witnessed many terrible air-raids. The tragic burning of the London docks was a sight indelibly imprinted in our memories. We turned the lights out, removed the blackout screening and stood watching the frightful picture. St. Paul's Cathedral and the City spires stood out, now visible against the lurid blaze, then rapidly obscured for a time by the blinding smoke. The cathedral's dome turned scarlet as we watched, glowing with the reflection of the merciless conflagration of the docks and the surrounding City. There were many such nerve-racking experiences while at the Langham Hotel and elsewhere. The night Broadcasting House was bombed was one of complete disorganization of the hotel services; lights went out, water mains were hit, and chaos followed during the ensuing search for an alternative means of light. Apparently an emergency lighting plant had been prepared, but that too failed. Candles were eventually placed on landings and stairways, all impromptu the first time, but successive onslaughts were met with a splendid and well-thought-out organization. It all went to show, Henry said, that we did not yet believe that there could be such a thing as total war on a civilian population. We never went to a shelter or to a cellar but always remained where we happened to be when an air-raid began. I used to read aloud to Henry, although at times, I fear, a little incoherently when a bomb seemed too threateningly near or Henry's interpolation of "My!" or "That was a whopper!" intruded. Then he would add: "Go on, dear Jessie, I love to hear your voice and we are together—so what else matters."

Some time later I found Henry's firm handwriting on a programme dated Saturday 17 August. "One peaceful day," he had noted laconically. Such little asides showed me the pent-up emotion behind Henry's calm exterior. He would not have me out of his sight for a moment. If I slipped out of Queen's Hall during a morning rehearsal and across the road to the Langham to prepare him a warm bath and see that the luncheon menu provided the right kind of food for the rest which must follow, I would wait at the window just to see what I knew would happen. The second the rehearsal ended Henry would come hurrying to the hotel, a searching eye uplifted for me and a fist waggling at me for having left him.

All the old *joie-de-vivre* returned now that the concerts had matured. Although an eight weeks' season was announced, Mr. Hitler closed us down on Saturday 10 September, after only four weeks. Joan Tribe and Benno Moiseiwitsch were Henry's colleagues that night, with the London Symphony Orchestra. Happily enough, a new work had figured in the programme, which Bax's *London Pageant* appropriately closed. Incidentally, fourteen first performances were included in that season. Henry's policy had always insisted on *first* performance. He fought the newer elastic programming of such items as 'First Concert Performance', 'First Performance in London', and greatly deplored the inclusion of suites assembled from composers' film music, or ballet, which he averred were not legitimate first performances. "If you allow this to go on, you will gradually find that composers will not bother to write a completely new work for the Promenade Concerts," he maintained. Nor did he approve of a guest-conductor-composer unless he was directing a real first performance. "We should have every composer asking to direct his work, never mind its age; and if we start opening up in this way, who is to decide whether it is right to invite Mr. A. and yet not Mr. Z.?" he said. "Go on with this intrusion and the eight weeks' season of Promenade Concerts can be directed by composers, simply leaving an item here and there for a representative of the dead."

Some of Henry's happiest hours at this time were spent at the Royal Academy of Music with the students of his senior orchestra. The attendance was remarkable, for most of these young people were engaged on war duties of one kind or another. Two-hour sessions were instituted, with no interval, to enable the students to travel home in daylight. It amused Henry when the treasurer of the R.A.M. suggested that as he would only be conducting for two hours instead of three, they proposed reducing his fee by one-third.

Henry wrote back, of course, in agreement. But he could not resist the temptation of reminding them that they were surely making musical history by engaging a conductor to wag the stick by the hour. The fee was twelve guineas for the three-hour rehearsals, and that Henry had insisted upon. Otherwise, he said, would-be conductors would feel it unfair of Wood to train the orchestra without a fee, and Henry, first and last, was a loyal and staunch professional. So, much as he would have liked to give his services in the name of future orchestral players, he resolved to stick to this small fee—and eight guineas it became during the war.

The R.A.M. held a memorial concert for Henry in the Duke's Hall on 1 December 1944, directed by Sir Adrian Boult and Henry's old friend, Ernest Read. The students played wonderfully well, but it shocked me, as it did many of Henry's friends who were present, to note the exclusion of Henry's orchestration of the National Anthem, in which he firmly believed—by his Alma Mater, his students' orchestra, to which he had given twenty-one years of devoted, disciplined service—less than four months after his death. Poor old Henry, he would have shrugged his shoulders and said: "Just like 'em."

CHAPTER 5

Raids

THE BLACKOUT, RAID warnings and actual raids had now become part of our life, and, looking back, it is difficult to speak calmly of the great emotional strain which marked the journeys Henry made in pursuit of his determined avowal to keep things going for orchestras, musicians and public alike.

Naturally, the upheaval in all our lives had immense repercussions on the financial side of concert-planning. In the early days of the war, if the raids were bad the public stayed at home. As the years went on, however, it seemed that music was the great solace and halls were nightly filled. But early on the box office suffered—although all the financial commitments had to be made in advance.

This problem was behind one big clash which marked the 1940 Promenade Concerts. Mr. Douglas insisted that artists must reduce their fees because of the uncertain box-office returns. Henry refused absolutely to implement this decision, and dissociated himself entirely from any such suggestion. The dispute came to a head over Solomon, whom Henry wished to be given at least three engagements during the projected eight-week season. Henry found himself in complete agreement with Mr. Mitchell, Solomon's manager, who was opposed to accepting the management's proposal. The outcome was that Solomon, for the first time in many years, was denied a Promenade Concert.

These were difficult times for the musicians themselves, uprooted as they were, often rehearsing and performing under difficult conditions, and finding engagements more difficult to obtain than before. To make them bear the brunt of war conditions by docking their fees would have been thoroughly unjust.

The Pilgrim Trust and the Carnegie Trust supported music very generously, and Henry Wood played his part by directing orchestral concerts for very small fees that barely covered his out-of-pocket expenses. Thus the L.S.O. and the L.P.O. were able to jog along. Whatever the fee, or if there was no fee at all, the programme was always approached by Henry with the same careful study, the same detailed attention to rehearsal and the same kindly understanding and encouragement towards the musicians of the orchestra and the solo artists. His calm control when raids and warnings disturbed the music-making during a concert communicated itself to the audience, who went on contentedly listening to the programme—although perhaps, like me, with one ear warily conscious of the 'noises off'.

Early in the war a suggestion was made which seemed a good one and keenly interested Henry, though I cannot remember who made it. The wartime restrictions on publicity and the difficulty of making a nation-wide appeal for anything but war charities or war bonds prevented him from putting it into effect—but the idea was to make the Henry Wood Promenade Concerts a nationally supported organization. According to the proposal, one shilling was to be subscribed annually by one million concert-goers. On this basis a national orchestra could be formed, to be used for the customary summer and winter seasons in London, and for some weeks in provincial cities where the activities of a resident orchestra would not be endangered or assailed. A wonderful idea, but a scheme that could not be born, let alone prosper, in wartime.

Belgium had bestowed the *Chevalier de l'Ordre de Couronne* upon Henry in 1920, and France had made him an *Officier de l'Ordre National de la Légion d'Honneur* in 1926, but he looked upon these honours as recognition of England's musical prestige, not Henry Wood's.

"I owe everything to the musicians of the orchestra," he said over and over again, and he meant it with all his heart. I wonder if some of his colleagues really knew and understood Henry Wood's utter disregard of self. It seems doubtful when one reads and hears the foolish references which float about from time to time now that he is no longer here. Someone wrote in one newspaper after his death: "For Henry Wood the rostrum was, amongst other things, a place where he exhibited his temperament for everybody to see, players and audience alike." How little did the writer know Henry! For him, gesture was an art in itself. "I paint a picture with my baton," he used to say. Temperament he had, of course, brimming over. But it was never paraded before the public eye or, indeed, privately. To have known his suffering under the strain of personal hurt, to have known his calm when he knew he was to leave us; then indeed one knew that Henry Wood's temperament was as disciplined and controlled as his application of it to music.

When he painted his picture with the baton there was never any doubt as to where the point of his stick was directed. There were no emotional flourishes but firm direction and a downbeat unmistakable even to the amateur. His eye was unavoidable and directed far more insistently than any emotional rostrum antics. His left-hand gesture was simple and to the point. That Henry did not emulate Weingartner's extremely confined beat does not mean that he did not appreciate the art with which that fine conductor 'painted his pictures'. Nor did he condemn the broad, fine gesture and definite baton line of the great Nikisch. He had seen all the great conductors of his youth, Steinbach, Mottl, Levy and others, and in later years he regarded Bruno Walter as the ideal painter of pictures. Every note a composer sets down on paper weaves a picture in his mind and it is left for the individual conductor or artist to visualize and interpret that picture. That is what Henry Wood meant when he said: "I paint a picture with my baton."

In *My Life of Music* Henry relates that he went abroad before he was seventeen to hear the leading musicians of the period and study their methods. There was none of the 'Bohemia' associated with the arts for Henry. His whole existence was one of exploration, seeking the authentic and traditional readings of the classics at as near first hand as was humanly possible. And how many new 'pictures' he visualized every year! In every season of Promenade Concerts came new works interwoven with the classical repertoire. Intrepid in the face of criticism, he brought to his young public all the newest works. In 1896 for instance, the second year of the Proms, he introduced the now famous *Scheherazade* suite and *Capriccio Espagnole* of Rimsky-Korsakov. What electrifying music it must have been in those days, for in these modernistic times it still remains new in its vivid friendliness. César Franck's *Le Chasseur Maudit* must also have been as 'modern' in 1897 as the most modern of the moderns now.

Henry was twenty-six when the first Promenade Concert opened at Queen's Hall. From that day he gave himself to the service of music and to teaching the public to know the panoramic pictures which music paints. His ideal was to bring music to a great public and in such an impeccable manner as to win those untutored thousands; yet, at the same time, to satisfy his own exacting musicianship backed by his personal contact with the great conductors of his youth.

A group of singers took part in the ill-fated 1940 Promenade season, and Henry's invitation to them to appear at Queen's Hall proved to be the inception of the Alexandra Choir. The story of these singers really dates back to a Handel festival concert on 3 June 1939. The Alexandra Palace organ in the Great Hall had been neglected and had never been tuned to French low pitch. Henry was asked to arrange a Handel festival at the Palace to defray the expense of reconditioning the organ. "Of course," he replied. But how? "Well, I'll think of a way to keep expenses down and profits up."

Sir Stanley Marchant, then principal of the Royal Academy, and Sir Hugh Allen, then principal of the Royal College of Music, agreed that the students of the senior orchestra and the students of singing should take part. Local choirs trained by Charles Proctor, supported by students from the Royal schools, formed the chorus which was named the Alexandra Palace Festival Choir. Isobel Baillie, Frank Titterton, Harold Williams and Margaret Balfour sang the solo parts in excerpts from *Israel in Egypt*, *Judas Maccabeus* and the *Messiah*. The box-office receipts provided enough money to pay for the reconditioning of the fine Willis organ, retuning it to French low pitch.

During the preliminary rehearsals for this concert, Henry noticed how capably the young chorus-master handled his singers. Later, he invited Mr. Proctor to bring a contingent of the choir to Queen's Hall—and the Alexandra Choir was born. It is a pity that the Alexandra Palace could not be refurbished to take the place of the lost Crystal Palace. The Great Hall is acoustically excellent and seats several thousands. If a gallery were built all round it would be a wonderful concert hall for choral concerts and, being within fifteen minutes of King's Cross, it is an ideal setting. It would provide musical organizations with a venue costing much less than the London concert halls.

It was during the rehearsals for those concerts in Alexandra Palace that Henry was delighted to come across one of his parents' relatives unexpectedly. Henry often expressed regret that he had been unable to keep in touch with distant members of his family. There was no reason for this lapse apart from the fact that his whole mind was absorbed by music, so that leisure for the enjoyment of social intercourse with his parents' relatives and friends was denied him.

Lieut.-Colonel Farley was chairman of the committee formed to carry out the scheme for the reconditioning of the organ at Alexandra Palace. One day he attended a rehearsal for the Handel festival and gave into Henry's hands a little photograph of a small boy in kilt and doublet, complete with sporran.

"Why," said Henry, "where on earth did you get this? I remember my mother had one. It is of myself when about four years old."

"I am a relative," replied Lieut.-Colonel Farley, "or rather my wife is a relative of your parents, and we have the original plate. I will send it to you if you like." Henry was thrilled, but, as always, the choir awaited him and with them off went his personal self to music again. Pressure of work and the war, which soon interfered with so many activities, prevented our making a further effort to meet again and explore the relationship. Nevertheless, it was a happy memory for Henry, and I know that Lieut.-Colonel and Mrs. Farley attended the ceremony of the unveiling of the memorial window dedicated to Henry in St. Sepulchre's Church after the war.

On another occasion in Manchester, I remember well how

Henry went to Armstrong's, in Deansgate, to purchase a new cord for his eyeglasses, and asked:

"Is Mr. Armstrong here?"

"No," was the reply, "but I can ask him to come along and see you when you come in to collect your glasses." And Henry was delighted a few days later to meet his cousin, Mr. A. Armstrong, now an architect, and later on to greet Miss Amy Armstrong. They are relatives on his father's side of the family. Miss Amy Armstrong sent me the family tree from the old family Bible.

Throughout his life all Henry's personal wishes and hopes of necessity gave place to heavy demands in the name of music, until it became too late to gather up the threads of any social existence. That was never more true than during the war years. Sometimes, however, he was given tangible evidence of the response to the joy he brought to a wider family circle—his musical public.

One intrepid member of the audience during the noisy 1940 Promenade Concerts was Joseph Kennedy, at that time American Ambassador to London. When the concerts were stopped by the air raids, Mr. Kennedy wrote to Henry, and I quote from his letter:

"The pleasure your concerts gave me was perhaps the most satisfying thing I experienced this sorry autumn. I had anticipated more weeks of thorough enjoyment. I shall miss them and your conducting."

Many were the nights when he, together with the packed Queen's Hall audience, remained to enjoy the impromptu concerts which Basil Cameron, the orchestra and artists carried on so long as a raid continued. I recall that the first air attack came on a Saturday afternoon. Henry insisted on going into Portland Place. With his usual inquisitiveness, he wanted to see 'how the thing worked'. Crowds gathered to watch what seemed to be a dog-fight over the East End. But that same night we were left in no doubt about the horrors of air warfare. The raids grew worse and, as already mentioned, the concerts had to cease on 10 September. On the following day we went to stay with friends for a few days at Great Missenden and from their friendly hospitality we moved, three days later, to a furnished house at Hyde Heath. Here, we were still subjected to bombing attacks night after night, an ordeal made more anxious because we had my son-in-law with us, gravely ill. On making local inquiries we discovered that the house we had rented had already suffered from bombing and that we were in a vulnerable position with searchlight units all around us.

I cannot leave these wartime memories without recalling a more amusing incident. I had written to the Board of Trade seeking a supplementary allocation of clothing coupons in order to purchase more woollen undergarments for Henry. The heavy exertion of rehearsal and conducting during the Promenade season meant that he required as many as twelve or fourteen sets of underclothes a week. "We are sending eight coupons for Sir Henry Wood," the Board of Trade replied. At that period, the eight coupons were sufficient for a single set of woollen underwear, a fact of which I reminded the Board when I wrote back. I pointed out, at the same time, that the request was on behalf of Sir Henry Wood, conductor of the Promenade Concerts.

This second letter merely drew the response that "all dance band leaders are allowed the same number of coupons".

CHAPTER 6

A Hard Winter—the 1941 Proms

SEVERAL CONCERTS DUE to take place in the north at this time had to be cut out as Henry really needed to squeeze some rest into his busy wartime programme. Happily we were able later on to fulfil engagements for concerts under the Pilgrim Trust sponsorship. We spent four days with friends on the way to Bristol for a B.B.C. concert during this period. In Bristol a full house in Colston Hall echoed the spirit of London in refusing to be done out of music by three air-raids. Then we set out for Manchester, where we settled down to a long series of concerts with the Hallé Orchestra in Manchester itself and elsewhere north. They lasted from 19 October 1940 until 20 January 1941. We spent Christmas Day with our dear friends, Mr. and Mrs. Bertram Thomas, at Bowden. It was during one of our visits to these friends—a party, in fact, for Henry's birthday—that we met their young evacuees, six boys of about ten or eleven years old. The children lived in one part of the house but apparently were allowed in the kitchen by the servants. While dinner was in the process of cooking, each boy chose the portion of food he wanted if any 'leftovers' came out of the dining-room. One boy had his eye on the savoury—creamed mushrooms on toast. At the time we knew nothing of this, of course. There was ample provision for the eight or ten guests, and one portion was left on the dish. After much pressing from our insistent hostess, Henry ate it. When the butler took out the empty dish he explained to the boy that none was left as Sir Henry Wood had eaten the last one. To which the little boy exclaimed in disgust: "And 'im a Sir!"

What frightful havoc there was in the Christmas raids on Manchester and district in 1940! Yet, as buoyant and determined as London and other cities, Manchester went about its business despite the extreme vulnerability of the factories and residential quarters concentrated in the city. It is interesting to look back at the desk diary Henry kept at this time and note the insertions made in his own handwriting. For instance, a programme of Sibelius works is down for January 1941 with the B.B.C. at Bristol. It was a programme he loved, and over my note of the engagement he wrote in pencil 'Sibelius'. That was just his method of expressing special pleasure. Months might pass without his making a mark on the bald list of daily engagements—until there came a birthday, a visit to a theatre, or a meeting with some treasured friend. Then, against the name, he would write 'What-ho!'. That always seemed to express the highest pitch of anticipation and pleasure.

It was in this year that the Hallé Orchestra committee invited Henry to become their permanent conductor but after careful consideration he declined. John Barbirolli— now Sir John—later took up the post, and faced a difficult task in those days of money restrictions. That a musician of such staunch idealism had been chosen by the Hallé Society gave Henry a deep satisfaction, and he was delighted that John accepted.

"Another one up for the Royal Academy of Music," purred Henry. "One of these days I should like to have a party— and what a big gathering it would be—of men and women whose names are now household words, all of them from my old Alma Mater." The difficulties of war prevented that party being held, but as usual 'what-ho' expressed Henry's happiness as he turned the project over in his mind. John Barbirolli was a past student at the R.A.M.

After German bombs destroyed Queen's Hall, burying decades of memories in heaps of rubble and depriving Londoners of their greatest concert hall, Henry quietly wrote in his desk diary under Sunday, 10 May 1941: "Easter Sunday was my last concert in Queen's Hall—*Parsifal*." There was no other comment, but the fact that he turned back the pages to insert this entry meant he felt something too deeply to discuss it. When Queen's Hall went his external calm, his almost unconcerned detachment, was a signal to refrain from sympathetic comment until months, perhaps years, had passed and the topic could be approached without arousing any visible show of emotion. Was it of prophetic significance that among that horrible devastation only Henry's bust still remained undamaged? This same bust I lend to the B.B.C. during the Henry Wood Promenade Concerts where it stands on the platform at the Royal Albert Hall beneath the organ.

Without the Queen's Hall and still ill at ease at the wartime change of management, Henry dreaded the approach of the 1941 Promenade season. Meanwhile, the Hallé Orchestra still claimed him, and many journeys and experiences during those concerts outside Manchester were endurance tests for a man of his age. I remember in Morecambe, on one of the many occasions when we went there with the Hallé Orchestra, finding a tiny bedroom, hot and stuffy, with the blinds drawn because corridor lights shone through a fanlight over the bedroom door and but for the drawn blinds would have shone out over the bay. Henry sat up most of the night with his head out of the window, having draped the blackout curtains over the back of his chair. "No more of this. I should suffocate," he said. So from then on, no matter what the hour or

weather, he travelled back to Manchester when he had finished
a concert in Morecambe or elsewhere in his work for the
Hallé. Northern weather in winter can be difficult enough
over hills and fells in normal times. Along dark roads, with
only a glimmer of car-lighting in the blackout, amid snow,
rain and fog, it was infinitely worse. Tucked up in rugs, Henry
would sometimes sleep or discuss the playing. But usually he
was so tired after the day's journey that he was content just
to inquire from time to time: "Are we getting near home,
dear Jessie?" Although the long, dark, cold journeys proved
exacting, Henry thoroughly enjoyed music-making with the
Hallé Orchestra. He enjoyed the northern public and their
studied enthusiasm for orchestral music. He was delighted
when visiting Workington and Carlisle on a Sunday in January
to note the huge cinema in the former town crowded to overflowing in the afternoon, and the hall in Carlisle, to listen to
the following programme:

Carneval Romain	*Berlioz*
Theme and Variations from 3rd Suite	*Tchaikovsky*
Symphony No. 3	*Brahms*
Coriolan	*Beethoven*
Symphony No. 4	*Mozart*
Scherzo from Midsummer Night's Dream	*Mendelssohn*
Ride of the Valkyrie	*Wagner*

All his discomforts during these journeys were well worth it
to see those great audiences.

One journey by road from Morecambe to Bristol some days
in advance of a Sibelius broadcast is memorable not only for
the frightful weather but for the reason we made it. Henry
had decided to invite the B.B.C. to accept the return of the
Promenade Concert seasons from 1942 onwards. He met Sir

Adrian Boult, who was permanent conductor of the B.B.C. Symphony Orchestra and the B.B.C. head of music, Mr. Julian Herbage, assistant in the music department, and Mr. W. W. Thompson, now concert manager of the B.B.C., who had begun his career in Queen's Hall under the one and only Robert Newman management.

Over an unhappy lunch on 14 January 1941 it became plain that the B.B.C. was in no mood to accept the proffered gift with open arms. "So difficult to assemble . . . difficulties regarding the orchestra . . . doubtful whether the B.B.C. Symphony Orchestra could come to London . . . problem of artists all so difficult"—the sad phrases hung in the air. No musical thought, no regard for a great musical institution—a national heritage for nearly half a century—seemed to move the speakers. It was curious, as Henry remarked, that at one time the B.B.C. were so anxious to emulate these concerts that they announced Promenade Concerts under the direction of Sir Adrian Boult in Manchester Opera House. The title 'Promenade Concerts' was, however, dropped for 'Summer Concerts' or some such name when Henry criticized the doubtful wisdom of using the term while they still sponsored the original Queen's Hall Promenade Concerts. He reminded them that it was simply asking other promoters to cash in on the title.

Henry left Bristol somewhat puzzled. The line of discussion had been utterly vague, and the whole atmosphere one of a tip-toe approach, presumably intended to leave the impression that his proposal would receive attention but leaving open a definite line of retreat.

The destruction of Queen's Hall in May 1941 certainly made it easier for the B.B.C. eventually to accept Henry's gesture in returning his Promenade Concerts to their sponsorship, for as well as the hall itself the German bombs wiped out a long history of complicated relations over its letting between Messrs. Chappell (Lessees) and the B.B.C., and it was easier for the B.B.C. to take over concerts held in the Royal Albert Hall. Henry had already pencilled the Royal Albert Hall for the 1942 and 1943 Promenade seasons, long before anyone had a chance to forestall him. Then came protracted negotiations, opening with a long and very happy talk with the then Controller of Programmes, Mr. B. E. Nicolls (now Sir Basil Nicolls) over lunch at the Hyde Park Hotel on 11 August 1941. This was, as ever when discussing anything with him, straightforward and minus comments, and although Henry felt somewhat frustrated he nevertheless knew that his wonderful gesture had not fallen on unsympathetic ground. Top-line discussions were soon on foot—but it took an exasperating time to come to a conclusion, and not until 11 February 1942 did the B.B.C. come to final acceptance and formally take over Henry's assignment.

There was no one happier than B. E. Nicolls at this time, and then, as after Henry's death, I found in him a very helpful and much cherished friend. I know, too, that once the return of the Proms was an accomplished fact, Henry had forgotten all his miseries of 1939-1941. In relating the data of these years, as with other episodes not as happy as could be desired, I am merely giving a factual account of Henry's daily life exemplifying his selfless devotion to music.

I remember so well how greatly touched Henry was on this February morning when Mr. Thompson, Mr. Herbage and Dr. R. S. Thatcher came to see us at the Hyde Park Hotel to advise him that all was settled for the take-over of his Promenade Concerts for the season 1942. He realized that Dr. Thatcher had set aside his private grief, having just been notified of the death in action of his only son, an Air Force casualty, to attend to what he knew was of much moment to Henry and the B.B.C. At this time Dr. Thatcher was associated with the music department of the B.B.C.

The long negotiations troubled Henry very much but happily the B.B.C. were quite ready to accept me as proxy, so I was able to shoulder all the preliminary discussions, only bringing to Henry matters which required his assent and confirmation. During these negotiations, before they had reached a cut-and-dried stage, I approached Mr. Holt, knowing as I did that Henry's health would not much longer stand the strain of protracted discussion regarding this matter, which seemed to him to be a very straightforward, unequivocal and generously forgiving gesture. I asked Mr. Holt whether he would be prepared to undertake the sponsorship of the Proms should the B.B.C. again withdraw. He at once agreed, and most kindly said he would find the required capital and that Henry need not be bothered by any of the business details but should give himself up to the music. That was a great comfort to Henry, one which neither he nor I forgot.

Henry had stood guarantor up to a certain amount during the Keith Douglas-Owen Mase management, and the six-weeks' 1941 season brought in about £17,000 from the box-office and programme sales. Broadcasting rights added to that figure. In 1942, when the B.B.C. resumed sponsorship, an eight-weeks' season brought together a paying public of 172,337 and the box-office receipts amounted to some £26,000 plus programme sales. During this season there were, of course, nightly broadcasts with Basil Cameron and Henry in command. The London Philharmonic Orchestra, the London Symphony Orchestra and the B.B.C. Symphony Orchestra shared the platform in succession.

In 1941 Stanley Rubinstein became honorary secretary of

the Proms Circle—an enthusiastic gathering together of Prommers founded in 1933 by Mr. E. H. Booking. Stanley Rubinstein gave much of his time and unbounded enthusiasm to this musical circle from which he was obliged to resign under pressure of work in 1951. In January 1944 the Proms Circle gave a dinner in honour of their president—Sir Henry—which was attended by 350 members. It was at this dinner that Henry gave the circle permission to assume the title of The Henry Wood Proms Circle. After Henry's death I suggested Dame Myra Hess as president, and until 1953 Dame Myra interested herself in that capacity in the circle's activities. On Dame Myra's resignation, Cyril Smith and Phyllis Sellick became co-presidents—and Sir Malcolm Sargent honoured the Circle by becoming their patron. The Circle carry on their meetings every Friday and every last Saturday of the month during the season October to April inclusive. Mrs. Jameson was elected honorary secretary on Mr. Rubinstein's resignation.

The forty-ninth season in 1943 gave Henry much pleasurable anticipation, for the B.B.C. decided to run it for nine weeks, with the London Philharmonic Orchestra for four weeks and the B.B.C. Symphony Orchestra for the remaining five. The box-office returns were £35,000 odd, plus programme sales and season tickets, although the last six nights were limited to a certain number of people owing to blackout regulations with the ending of Summer Time. Nightly broadcasts again brought these concerts to a vast listening public. It leaves no doubt as to the financial results that would have been shown in Henry's jubilee year of 1944 had not the flying bombs shut us down after the first three weeks. While receipts were encouraging—many thousands per week is required to run these concerts—what pleased Henry particularly was the fine response to the B.B.C.'s return to management of The Proms. It was heartening to see that fine hall filled each night under war conditions with an audience which included a good proportion of Services men and women both British and American.

But to return to January 1941 when Henry and I travelled over so much of England by road. It was memorable for the extraordinarily bad weather, particularly during one journey from Manchester to London. Roads were blocked by snow-drifts as high as the car. The first couple of times we had to be dug out of such drifts Henry was amused, but finally we were so cold we decided to put in at Lichfield. Not a room was available in the several hotels, all of them being full to the brim with travellers in the same predicament as ourselves. We did not look forward to sitting up all night, and the effect on Henry's health would have been serious after the trying journey. "Let's find the organist of the cathedral; he may know of someone in the neighbourhood," I suggested.

That kind colleague, Dr. Henry Porter, came immediately to the hotel in answer to Henry's telephone call, insisting that we stay with him and declaring that his wife would be happy to be of service in this emergency. Though we declined to impose upon him, we found it a very delightful interlude to have tea with him and his wife in their lovely old-world home under the shadow of the cathedral. Henry found it hard to express his gratitude for the renewed invitation to remain there at least for the night and, though formal in his thanks, a sniff, a quick attack with a handkerchief to the nose, denoted the moist eyes which were always Henry's little sign of suppressed emotion. Through the good offices of our host, however, the hotel 'found' us a room and we remained in the city two or three days, not only on account of the weather but because Henry wanted to see every inch possible of that lovely cathedral and the beautiful old city.

This reminds me of another mid-winter drive, this time from London to Manchester. We were ascending a hill out of Lichfield on the north side when we came into a dark, thick fog. Driving through the denseness I suddenly had to brake on account of what seemed to be a huge white patch, rather like the ghost of a horse. It was no ghost, however, but a sixteen-hander, pure white with long mane and tail. The creature was completely lost and petrified with fright at the approaching side-lamps of the car. We got out of the car and safely deposited the terrified animal in a meadow which it was evidently trying to find.

The friendly spirit and the enthusiasm of Bradford compensated for the terrifying approach to the rostrum in East-brook Hall there, down fifteen or sixteen of the steepest steps to grace any public hall. I am sure that if it had not been for the spirit that prevailed at those Bradford subscription concerts, and the musical satisfaction the players of the Hallé Orchestra always afforded Henry, those steps would have found Henry 'otherwise engaged'.

Henry always looked forward to his concerts in Bradford. The committee, under the chairmanship of H. P. Ambler, included a well-known northern name associated with the support of music not only in Bradford but also in Manchester and Liverpool—H. J. Behrens—and Mr. Meanwell Henton, L.R.A.M., was the most indefatigable of honorary secretaries. The latter was most kind in his preparations for what comfort could be afforded Henry during these wartime visits. Once, on arrival in Bradford, we found that one of our suitcases had not been put on the train. Of course, it contained Henry's dress suit. He amused his evening audience with a little speech about the missing case and asked them to forgive his 'costume'.

Another Bradford experience was not of such a lighthearted character. Up early after a fine concert the previous night, Henry suddenly became ill. I realized at once what it was and sent for a doctor, telling him by phone that it had been a slight seizure. Dr. Cunningham, I think it was, carefully examined Henry and advised a few days in bed without moving from the city. But Henry wanted to be home, and so I drove him back by road, propped up carefully in rugs and pillows. Our own doctor was summoned and in a few days he recovered; but it was a great anxiety trying always to keep at bay that terrific enthusiasm and energy without damping his fine, hopeful spirit.

The Good Friday *Parsifal* concert from the B.B.C. studio found him again regretting his *Parsifal* 'Mushroom Bells' which had been destroyed in the blitz of Queen's Hall. Over forty years earlier Henry had personally supervised the casting of the first four of the very large hemispherical bells at the Shoreditch bell foundry of Mears and Stainbank. Later, the firm completed an octave of the Mushroom Bells, creating an instrument of magnificent tone which Henry had found of the greatest value for all works containing important bell parts and in which he took a personal pride. For forty years the bells, which later had been purchased by the B.B.C., stood in an alcove by the organ in Queen's Hall.

They were badly missed at the *Parsifal* concert on 11 April, when the B.B.C. Symphony Orchestra was a group torn between being working musicians and Home Guard. Many of them had been through harrowing experiences. Paul Beard had narrowly escaped death, as had several members of the orchestra. Sidonie Goossens and Jessie Hinchliffe lost all their belongings. Their spirit was wonderful but the tense strain was, I think, worse in Bristol than in London. Bristol was not only a vulnerable spot, but very concentrated, and air attacks seemed more intense in that confined city.

Apart from the Royal Academy Orchestra rehearsals, which of course continued this year as in others, Henry greatly enjoyed his 'Scrapbook' broadcast, in which John Gielgud also appeared. Henry was always co-operative and willing to give all the time a producer needed when he took part in such activities, and in him Mr. Leslie Bailey found an ideal subject.

It was the same with a photographer. Henry would give all the time and help required, with that interest of his in all subjects in which he was not well versed. He was learning always, anything and everything, so that life for him was a new book of fresh interest every day, never stale or dull, and with never an idle minute.

Yet he would not read newspapers unless some incident in music, art or science was brought to his notice. I doubt if he would ever have known much of the sad or brutal things—murders and so forth—happening in the world if someone had not discussed reports of them during conversation with him. So aloof was he from the daily Press that I urged him to read either *The Times* or *Daily Telegraph* leaders during the war. This he did because it was asked of him. But throughout the war I do not remember even a single comment, much less a discussion, on the progress of our arms, except about the weary length of the war for everybody. The prospect of getting back to work on projects he had in mind—performances of *Parsifal*, Mahler's Second and Eighth Symphonies, Elgar's works, particularly *Gerontius*, now one of Sir Malcolm Sargent's finest interpretations, and worthwhile new music—and plans for them all filled his thoughts, and the war stood in the way. But his attitude should not be misconstrued as indifference to the tragedies and battles that daily disturbed the world. Henry cared, cared too much, and preferred to hope every day that the carnage and suffering might end. Every day he was brought into contact with some eighty-five to a hundred musicians, none of whom wholly escaped the blows of the war. All too frequently there was the death of a son, a husband or a father to mourn—and all were related to 'Timber', and always the news was received with a furtive tear.

Of course, Henry performed many new works, despite the war, and numbers of them are now on the high road to safe inclusion in the repertoire. Ralph Hawkes, who died very suddenly in New York at an early age, was then a partner in the music-publishing firm of Boosey and Hawkes. He drew Henry's attention to several works, among them those of Rubbra. Henry liked this young man's music—the composer was then still in his early thirties—and Rubbra must be grateful for the interest which Henry took in his compositions.

The 1941 Promenade Concerts ran the full six weeks as planned, opening on 12 July at the Royal Albert Hall and, as far as I remember, continuing undisturbed by any warlike activity in the skies overhead. One outstanding happiness for Henry at these concerts was the appearance of Cyril Smith and Phyllis Sellick as partners in the *Carnival des Animaux* on the opening night. Henry had invited them to do this, fully realizing that it might sometimes mean effacement of individuality, but knowing they were a very devoted partnership as husband and wife. Cyril and Phyllis enjoyed their two-piano work and later often told Henry how grateful they were to him for the suggestion, since they not only adored it but were able to travel together, a joy denied them when each went a separate way for solo and concert engagements only. It pleased Henry, too, when Arthur Catterall partnered his daughter Audrey in Bach's Violin Concerto No. 3 in D minor, on 23 July. He retained memories of many concerts when Arthur Catterall was leader of the B.B.C. Symphony Orchestra, and this little family gathering gave him great delight.

There were many broadcasts from the Albert Hall during this 1941 season and attendances were remarkable throughout. As in Queen's Hall, 1940, so at the Royal Albert Hall the courage and tenacity of everyone was superb—and, if ever there was the slightest sign of nerves, Henry remained the centre from whom self-control and geniality beamed comfort into artists every day. I well remember Heddle Nash coming to rehearsal once, looking terribly shaken—his home had been bombed overnight—but he sang in his never-to-be-forgotten style with that voice of a quality of rare beauty—although, as he has since said, "I shook and trembled for a week." Can one ever forget the calm control with which Elena Danieli sang that lovely song of Berlioz, "Le Spectre de la Rose" while an alert was announced and 'doodles' soared overhead? What an artist she was, a protégée of Melba, and later on one of Henry's pupils—and withal a cultured French linguist. Dame Myra one remembers also, not only during the same Promenade Concert at the Albert Hall, but daily, many and many a time, at the National Gallery Concerts.

But it was an unhappy time musically for Henry, who hankered for a return to stable, disciplined management. He scented the divided loyalties among the many outside personalities who interfered during this season, and finally he found it difficult to keep his temper in check. "A Fred Karno set-up after all these years," he exclaimed.

It was then that Henry asked the B.B.C. to let him have Mr. W. W. Thompson as his personal manager (which they very generously did) and so cut out all approach to the Keith Douglas side of management. After preliminary talks with

Mr. Askew, then manager at the Albert Hall, Henry also pencilled certain weeks for 1942 and 1943 Promenade Concerts
and opened the way more surely for a return to B.B.C. sponsorship. I can see Henry now, tripping along, pattering nimbly
down those stone stairs at the Albert Hall after concluding this
arrangement with Mr. Askew. Leaving my more cautiously
negotiated descent far behind, Henry made for the street with
a broad smile and the rather heightened colour that denoted
the excitement the interview had caused him. Pushing his left
hand through his hair, he exclaimed as I caught up with him:

"Good! Now all's safe for the fiftieth [Promenade Season]
anyway, and I hope for the B.B.C. too."

CHAPTER 7

Reunited with the B.B.C.

ON 11 FEBRUARY 1942, after all the preliminaries had been settled, the British Broadcasting Corporation signed the contract which Henry had negotiated for the Royal Albert Hall. Thus the B.B.C. resumed management of the Henry Wood Promenade Concerts. Henry sought no material reward for his gesture to the Corporation. He had no interest in finance, much less in bargaining over the value of his work. It was enough for him that his concerts were back, safely cradled for another fifty years. Henry hoped the B.B.C. really understood the enormous value of the gift he brought them. With the Queen's Hall in ruins, the Albert Hall had become the only building in London capable of housing Promenade audiences, and it was little wonder that Henry soon became feverishly anxious to ensure that the hall was booked well ahead for the 1944 season—the fiftieth anniversary season. He was eager not for his own glorification but to make sure that the most was made of this landmark in order to protect the future of the concerts and the continuation of the musical education of the young people for whom the Proms so especially cater.

The leisurely manner in which his wishes on this matter were received perturbed and ruffled him, the more so since he felt sure that in handing the Proms back to the B.B.C. he had presented the Corporation with the finest possible musical shop window, an established wonder and envy the world over. This spirit of frustration shadowed his final agreement to make the B.B.C. curators of his life's work. But he felt it was safer for the sake of music that these concerts should go steadily on in continuity under a management well able to undertake the financial sponsorship.

The Sunday concerts of the late Harold Holt provided a welcome escape from these worries about the future. For these concerts Henry had a completely free hand in drawing up the programmes, which were designed so as to obtain the best results from a single rehearsal. No one was better than Henry at planning under these conditions, for whatever the work he could always tell you at once—"No, that's too difficult, there's always that ticklish passage for the oboe", or "that's something that doesn't come off without very close rehearsal".

Without reference to the score he knew at once what the orchestra required, even though he might not have seen the work for ten years. One of these Sunday concerts was specially memorable. It was the centenary of the birth of Sullivan, who was born on 14 May 1842 at Bolwell Terrace, Lambeth, and died on St. Cecilia's Day (22 November) 1900. Henry prevailed on Harold Holt to allow him to give once again that lovely work *The Golden Legend*, with Joan Hammond, Astra Desmond, Henry Wendon, Dennis Noble and the Alexandra Choir.

To Muriel Brunskill went the famous *Lost Chord*, and grandly she sang it that afternoon. Henry was again sad about the loss of his beautiful Mushroom Bells, for they were so full of that rich quality, demanded in the fine prologue, which is lacking in ordinary tubular bells.

In May 1942 John Barbirolli came to the Royal Academy of Music to read a telegram from Toscanini addressed to Henry, Myra Hess and Sir Adrian Boult congratulating them on their wartime work for music. This same day Henry was again giving his devoted interest to the future of Bandmaster Needham. In 1937, Henry and I had been walking on the garden front of the hotel at Broadstairs in which we were then staying for a little rest after a dental operation, when we heard in the distance the strains of a military band playing *The Flying Dutchman*. "My!" exclaimed Henry, cocking his head on one side with that quick repeated shake which always accompanied intense listening. "That's good. Whoever he is, he knows Wagner. Let's go and see what it is." It turned out to be the band of The Royal Berkshire Regiment playing in the gardens, and we stood on the edge of the crowd to listen. Henry commented on the unusually free method of conducting, unlike the accepted military style. The *Tannhauser* overture followed, given with the same markedly perceptive direction.

Henry was impressed: "That's what we want to teach the public—that there is more than just four square beats in a bar," he said. "There's poetry, there's a picture, and the pictures Wagner painted were of human emotions—life. I'm glad we heard this man."

Five years later a lady interested in Bandmaster Needham came to see Henry to discuss the possibility of a civilian position for him when his term of service expired. Eventually this enthusiastic musician was placed in charge of the police band in Manchester. I believe he is still there, and he later started the Salford Symphony Orchestra, derived mainly from keen amateur musicians. This progress was just what pleased Henry, for he spent much of his time giving advice and thought to every applicant. His great idea was to surmount obstacles and get on, and this is one of many such instances.

Just before the opening of the 1942 Promenade Concert

season, Henry broadcast Shostakovich's Seventh Symphony, the *Leningrad*, from the B.B.C. studio on 22 June. This turned out to be a terrific undertaking, for the score was delayed in the wartime journey from Russia and when it did reach England there were days and days of work for the copyists. Then so many errors were discovered in the score and orchestral parts that Messrs. Novello sent a copyist to Henry for several days of intense work. Henry was hard at it right through the day and almost into the night as well, striding backwards and forwards to his desk consulting his copyist, and his heightened colour made me fearful lest this strain should result in a breakdown, for he had not been too well. I was quite wrong, however, and should have relied on the interest of this new work to keep everything at bay, at any rate until its performance. The Russian ambassador and Mrs. Maisky attended this world broadcast of the *Leningrad* symphony. It was a huge success and of course the London Symphony Orchestra responded nobly, feeling with Henry the thrill of this message from England through the medium of the fine work of a Russian composer. We all believed that night that we were sending to the world a declaration of friendship sealed through the trials of a war endured side by side.

Timing the work, Henry decided it ran to about seventy minutes. "No good, Sir Henry, we cannot get it into any other period," the anxious B.B.C. programme-planners replied. "Sixty minutes must be the limit, or we shall overrun the nine o'clock news."

How Henry sweated over this, cutting short the intervals and closing in on passages where he would have liked a little less rigidity! Many who took part in the broadcast will remember how for once Sir Henry Wood was not offended by the studio clock. He invariably requested that all clocks be covered during a rehearsal or a concert, preferring to rely upon his own timing of a work and a glance once in a while at his own repeater. But on this occasion he looked straight up at the huge studio clock and could hardly wait for the red light to fade before he said with great glee and a broad smile: "We've done it! And not a second either way." Even as he spoke, the chimes of Big Ben had taken the place of Shostakovich's music and listeners' minds were turning to the latest war reports. Henry's dislike of a clock facing him while conducting was so intense that when he went to the provinces he would pack a green baize bag in his suitcase if he thought he might be conducting in a hall where his wishes were unknown. On arrival, he would have the baize covering placed over an offending timepiece.

The reception after this performance found Mr. and Mrs. Maisky full of gratitude, and all connected with that evening's performance must have felt that wars could not possibly occur if only people would concentrate on such right things. The performance also resulted in a charming letter from Mr. Cecil Graves, co-Director General of the B.B.C. He wrote:

"Broadcasting House, W.1
"23 June 1942

"Dear Sir Henry,

"I was going to write in a day or two to send you on behalf of the Corporation all good wishes for your forty-eighth season of Promenade Concerts which opens next Saturday, but after being present at Maida Vale last night I felt I must write at once to congratulate you on the performance of the Leningrad Symphony. I have no technical knowledge of music, but I realized immediately what it must have meant to produce at short notice and—as I understand—from none too good parts, such a magnificent rendering of this long and complicated new work.

"We are very grateful to you and to the London Symphony Orchestra which responded so splendidly to your inspiring leadership.

"May I now send you our good wishes for the season which starts on Saturday, when once again the B.B.C. renews its traditional close collaboration with you in the Promenade Concerts.

"Yours sincerely,
"Cecil Graves."

So full of admiration was Henry for the new Shostakovich work that he determined to substitute it for the Tchaikovsky Symphony No. 4 in E minor, scheduled in the prospectus for the first Monday of the Promenade season, and in this way Shostakovich's No. 7 received its first public performance in England on 29 June. It was received by a rapturously excited and thrilled public, and Mr. and Mrs. Maisky again attended, as enthusiastic as before.

Eighteen first performances figured in the eight weeks of the 1942 season, beginning with the *Epic March* by John Ireland on the opening night. What a 'house' and what enthusiasm! As for Henry—well, calm reassurance, and my heart is still grateful for the comfort which followed the agitation of the previous two years and the unnecessary anxiety which the autumn of 1939 and the early months of 1940 had given him. Henry was now grateful and full of understanding of the routine which was essential before the Corporation could sign the Royal Albert Hall contracts.

Another work which gave him much satisfaction in this season was the first performance of Moeran's Violin Concerto, with Arthur Catterall as soloist. Then came a Symphonic Poem, *Pannychis*, by Harry Farjeon; *Scherzo for Orchestra* by William Leonard Reed; *Dialogue for Pianoforte and Orchestra* by Elisabeth Maconochy; a pianoforte concerto by Alan Rawsthorne (with Louis Kentner as soloist); Alan Bush's Symphony in G; a Ballet Suite *Billy the Kid* by the American composer Aaron Copland; *Heroic Prelude* by William H. Harris (organist at St. George's Chapel, Windsor), and *Rondo for Orchestra* by Arthur Benjamin, deftly named *Prelude to Holiday*; *Three Idylls* for pianoforte and orchestra by Alex Rowley, with the composer as soloist; *Valses Graves et Gaies* by Norman Demuth; *Suite Francaise* by Leighton Lucas; Rubbra's Fourth Symphony; *Triptych, Three Expressions for Violin and Orchestra* by Thomas F. Dunhill, with Max Rostal as solo violin; *Circus Suite* by Mary Anderson Lucas; and Benjamin Britten's *Sinfonia da Requiem*, to complete this proud answer to total war. That this great hall could be filled every night to hear not only the comfortable reassuring works of the classica but to listen to less known and new works was a triumph. Even on the last night a new work—Ruth Gipps's symphonic poem *Knight in Armour*—received its first performance.

At the final concert on 22 August, after an uproarious reception for orchestra and conductor, Henry went forward and made this little speech:

"My dear friends, this brings our glorious season to a close. It has been one of extremely happy co-operation with my colleagues, Mr. Basil Cameron and Sir Adrian Boult, the London Philharmonic Orchestra and the B.B.C. Symphony Orchestra. Before bidding you adieu, I must thank you and tell you what a wonderful audience you are. How you listen! Your attention is so encouraging and exhilarating.

We look forward to meeting next year in this great old hall . . . I hope, (at this point the audience shrieked delight, and Henry paused before adding) I hope, in days of peace."

I have a record of this speech. Slow and calm, his voice revealed afresh his friendliness and utter freedom from self-consciousness. It was a memorable ending to a season which gave back to the nation this heritage of one man's dogged persistence for the sake of music.

It is easy to see now that one man could not continue to undertake the terrific strain of an eight-weeks' season of nightly concerts—six a week and rehearsals—and it is worth remembering that Henry instituted the first assistant-conductorship when he invited Basil Cameron to join him for the Promenade Concerts of 1940. When giving back his Promenade Concerts to the B.B.C. in 1942, Henry decided that, although he hoped Sir Adrian Boult would take a share with his B.B.C. Symphony Orchestra, Basil Cameron should retain his now acknowledged place. Sir Adrian wrote to Henry after the 1942 Prom season a letter from which I quote:

"24 August 1942

"My Dear Sir Henry,
    "I cannot leave London and the neighbourhood of the dear old Albert Hall, without writing you a word of thanks —however poor and inadequate—for all your kindness and consideration during this wonderful month. It has been a great experience for me, and I have learnt much from it, but I keep on harking back to forty-one years ago when you first began to teach me. I think I should have gone mad if any one had told me then that I should one day act as your assistant at the Proms! And it has really happened!

"I do hope that you have managed the move without too many of the vexations that always seem joined up with these affairs, and with my kind regards to you and Lady Wood from us both,

"Yours gratefully,
"Adrian Boult."

A few days at home straightening up music, answering scores of letters, a walk or two in Regent's Park and a little repose—then we were off once again on the autumn round. There were provincial concerts and others in Greater London and elsewhere with the L.P.O. and the L.S.O., still sponsored, of course, by the Pilgrim Trust and the Carnegie Trust. It was while he was on the platform at the Golders Green Orpheum with the L.P.O. that Henry's pockets and dressing-case were rifled. His watch, his money and a gold cigarette-case given him many years before by his old friend Sir Edgar Speyer were all stolen.

We had a remarkably beautiful concert in Salisbury Cathedral, with the L.P.O. once more, where to a packed 'congregation' was played:

Trumpet Voluntary	*Purcell-Wood*
Serenade to Music	*Vaughan Williams*
Symphony No. 8	*Beethoven*
Suite for Strings	*Rameau-Savage*
Enigma Variations	*Elgar*

"Ah," said Henry, when visiting Sir Walter Alcock during the short interval, "what a lovely life it must be to live in a quiet beautiful home in the close, sheltered by the cathedral, and to have a fine organ entirely your own!" Sir Walter was at that time eighty-one, but looked no more than sixty-five, the picture of health and happiness. They talked, those two, about the past, the unhappy present, and the future. One of Sir Walter's memories was of a visit to Henry's father in Oxford Street when he went to the shop to purchase some parts for an engine, a hobby with which he beguiled his spare moments. There he had found the owner of the shop perusing a score. "Goodness me," said Alcock, "you reading a score?" "Yes," replied Henry's father, "young Henry Wood is my son, and I have taught him quite a lot about music. He is at present away directing the orchestra on the Marie Roze tour."

Chatting there in Salisbury, Henry turned to Sir Walter and asked:

"Would you care to play one of the Handel-Wood concertos at the Promenade Concerts next year?"

"Wouldn't I just love it!" Sir Walter answered with delight. And play he did, on 4 August 1943. No. 10 in D minor was chosen, and it was a thrilling experience for these two old friends, Sir Walter aged eighty-three, and Henry seventy-three.

Henry revelled in a pageant which Ensa organized during 1942 under the title of *Cathedral Steps*. It was to be performed on the steps of St. Paul's Cathedral and repeated before all the blitzed cathedrals of Britain. It consisted of descriptive and incidental music by military bands. It did not matter to Henry that it was a bitterly cold day, that a rehearsal was planned for 8 a.m. on the steps of St. Paul's, or that he suffered a wretched cold in consequence. It was *Britain*, and Henry Ainley's golden voice and Dennis Noble's singing of *Songs of the Fleet* with the Alexandra Choir thrilled Henry so much that the resulting cold seemed worth it even to my jealous care.

At this time Henry began to notice that the strain of the

continued war years was having a marked effect on singers. The exacting, uncomfortable railway journeys, and the reaction of highly emotional characters to war incidents demanded physical endurance and nerves of steel if those little vocal cords, those utterly human instruments, were to survive. It worried him greatly to note that many a voice was becoming tired, a tremolo creeping into what had been a fine steady instrument. "What is going to happen to these dear singers?" he would ask, full of compassion, for he saw that the ordeal would leave a gap of years during which it would be pretty well impossible for an artist to build a reputation, even though he or she had sacrificed so much to keep the war effort going. In the 1942 Promenade Concert season twenty-eight singers appeared, some singing at two concerts, of whom I particularly mention Janet Howe. This young artist had been introduced to Henry by Harold Holt earlier in the year. Henry was greatly impressed by her singing of The Rondo (*La Cenerentola*) by Rossini. "A lovely voice and every note of that difficult aria clearly articulated," he said after the audition. "I've never heard it sung better."

An incident of the 1942 season was really very funny, although it was a flagrant disregard for propriety and discipline anyway, much more so since it was before an audience. I was horrified, yet at the same time terribly inclined to laugh myself, when a horn player suddenly shoved the bowl of his instrument on to the head of another player during Tchaikovsky's Symphony No. 5. When the interval came, Henry demanded an explanation, and received the reply:

"I was very angry, Sir Henry, he was playing so badly."

"Thank you," said Henry with cold dismissal, all the more freezing because of his usually kind understanding; but he told me afterwards that, angry as he felt, he had

had a hard job not to laugh because the sight had been so comical. This calls to my mind an incident in July 1944 when Henry was taking a rehearsal. Looking to the back desks he said: "Gentlemen, I notice you are smoking behind your stands, but I can see you. I thought only taxi-drivers smoked while doing their job." All cigarettes vanished. Benno Moiseiwitsch came on to rehearse and, taking off his jacket, sat at the piano and, as usual, lit a cigarette, whereupon came shouts from the orchestra "Taxi!—Taxi!"

CHAPTER 8

The 1943 Proms

IN 1943 I HOPED things would ease up and give Henry more rest. Rest! Looking back I know how difficult it was for him to do this. Given an hour of free time, he was either deeply bent on scoring or re-scoring a work, or engrossed in a book. The problem was to find that complete relaxation which his doctor had warned me to insist on; yet it was inadvisable to warn Henry himself. Any reading of his own choice was certainly a form of relaxation, but in name only, for he was up and down to the library for a reference here or there when something puzzled him or he doubted a statement. His mind was never at rest and that made for unseen and irksome hidden emotion. So I hoped he would agree and avoid too much activity during 1943, in order to conserve his strength for the Promenade jubilee the following year.

He sat many times for Frank O. Salisbury in January 1943, the result being a fine painting and a true portrait. A friend seeing the portrait for the first time remarked: "It's Henry inside and out." True, it was just all that, it was even a little frightening when I looked at the finished work, for there was an expression in the eye which clearly revealed that hidden, unspoken introspection which I had noted at odd times since his first slight illness—the illness which he had quietly recognized as a seizure. But to keep Henry *quiet* and *keep* him quiet was merely putting fire to the combustible material in his active mind. The suggestion "Stay in bed and read" sometimes worked for a time, but it usually ended by bringing the library to the bedside, complete with notes and screeds

124

accumulated for future reference or works for the next season's Proms or arias that "so-and-so must sing next year", and a period of intense work would follow.

However, an easier January ran into February, by which time he was already reading the scores of new works for the coming season. A visit, as Frank Salisbury's guest, to the Devonshire Club for lunch gave him much happiness. "I've always wanted to become a member of such a club," he said, as he told me of the men he had met, in particular Charles Tait, an old friend of mine and chief of the Lancashire Electric Power Company at that time, and of the welcome extended to him by the chairman, Ormond A. Blyth. Henry eventually was elected a member, to his great satisfaction.

I tried to restrict the Sunday concerts as much as possible, especially where much travelling in the blackout was involved. It was difficult, for I dared not keep a suggested date from Henry's knowledge. He always insisted that what was asked of him he should fulfil.

I did my utmost to wean him from Jay Pomeroy's invitation to direct ten or so concerts within a month at the Stoll Theatre but to no avail. As it turned out, however, these concerts proved a tonic to him and to his artistic sense. He found the theatre ideal for music-making, and Jay Pomeroy engaged artists of the first rank, together with the London Symphony Orchestra, announcing the concerts as "A Season of Music for the People".

A journey to Liverpool for a concert in aid of Lady Cripps's "Aid to China" Fund, due to take place on 13 March, had to be postponed as Yehudi Menuhin did not arrive on schedule, his plane having been held up owing to war restrictions. Consequently, other engagements had to be reshuffled—for, once Henry had given his word, nothing would make him go back on it. We rushed back to London for a Holt Sunday concert at the Albert Hall, though it was all too much of a strain under prevailing conditions.

All the same, Henry enjoyed every minute. Weary sometimes with the travelling and sometimes with the orchestra as well, he never blamed anyone. Tedious wartime working conditions and fatigue occasionally affected his spirit of resistance to the encroachment of lower standards, but it never dulled his musical sense. I firmly believe, however, that Rachmaninoff's death, announced on Sunday 28 March, saddened Henry deeply and did bring home to him a thought he never uttered, that of age. "No," he used to say, "never remember or speak of age. There is no such thing."

The "Aid to China" concert at Liverpool did not come off until 23 March, as, when Menuhin eventually arrived, other concerts had intervened. It was a great evening in the Liverpool Philharmonic Hall, when both Yehudi and Henry gave their services. Henry would always give his services for charity concerts, although he was strongly opposed to the cutting of fees in purely professional music-making. In the case of charity performances, he averred, the public should understand that if artists' fees had to be extracted from the box office the charity rarely received anything. What calls were made upon Henry's services in this way during the war!

I can see him bubbling over with merriment when the Hon. Leonard Cripps (Sir Stafford's brother) came on to the platform and told the crowded house of the reasons for the postponement. "But all is well now," Mr. Cripps said. "Mr. Menuhin is here, and Sir Henry, in spite of the many calls upon him, has travelled again to Liverpool. Here he is," he added as Henry walked on to the platform, "the old tough has delivered the goods." The National Anthem was sung with lusty gusto, in which Henry could feel the intense anticipation which Yehudi had brought to this tremendous house. The audience was not disappointed; the Mendelssohn and Elgar concertos found Menuhin in fine fettle. Henry and Yehudi had met only a few days before for a Red Cross and St. John's Fund concert at the Royal Albert Hall on 18 March, when the concertos were the Mozart in D major and the Brahms, with the London Philharmonic Orchestra. They met again on 4 April, when Menuhin played at a Harold Holt Sunday concert.

Then there was the concert in aid of the Royal Naval War Libraries on 14 April at the Albert Hall, with Myra Hess and the L.S.O.; and yet another charity concert for our Prisoners of War Fund, organized by the Mayor of Kensington, R. C. D. Jenkins, J.P., at which Solomon and Eva Turner appeared with the B.B.C. Symphony Orchestra on 15 May. Eva Turner's name recalls Henry's suggestion that it was about time her work—especially in her heyday—should receive some official recognition. "She took up the cudgels on England's behalf and stormed the house of Italian opera in its own home"— and he said: "Has ever her singing in *Turandot* been beaten?"

The Dream of Gerontius, for Good Friday, 23 April, as usual took every minute of Henry's free time and thought; but the first rehearsals with soloists and the Luton choir and several preliminary orchestral rehearsals made for a beautiful broadcast with the B.B.C. Symphony Orchestra.

The Easter Sunday concert, following so soon upon this pressure of work, tried Henry greatly. He was already looking tired and had to face a terrific programme with the then customary single rehearsal:

Symphony No. 1 in C	*Beethoven*
Piano Concerto No. 1	*Tchaikovsky*

Till Eulenspiegel	*Strauss*
Symphony No. 7 in A	*Beethoven*

Henry always said that Beethoven's No. 7 was the most tiring work to direct, with not a 'let-up' anywhere, and I am sure he did not change his opinion that day. We decided to get away quietly, if only for a few days, to my son-in-law's country home in Weston. On the way down Henry seemed preoccupied; he said he was cold, that was all, and he certainly did not look any more than tired. Suddenly, about one o'clock in the morning after our arrival, he insisted that a wind was blowing over his face—which was quite possible in the old oak-beamed house. I quickly obtained hot-water bottles and a screen with the help of that dear, kind family, but in half an hour a rigor intervened. Henry was soon delirious, sitting up in bed directing an orchestra, demanding attention in a stentorian voice such as no living orchestra had ever heard from him. We soon had our dear Dr. Skeggs in from Stevenage, who in turn asked Lord Horder to come, which of course he did, and with the efficient help of the local nurse managed to cope with that foretold breakdown.

For ten days he was not ill. Oh no! Not Henry! He made progress to a kind of restful recovery, quite determined to be well enough to undertake the Red Cross concert, which we had been instrumental in making possible as a complete box-office gift to that grand institution. Once more Henry's iron determination triumphed and we returned to London on the eve of the concert with Henry well enough to conduct.

That was to have been his last public engagement before the opening of the Proms; his resolution was to rest quietly for a time. It had been a new experience to hear Henry say: "I won't do any more concerts until the Proms." It filled my heart with hope and some little comfort, for I dreaded the Proms season with Henry's health so delicately poised. But his wartime resolution was "No rest if the orchestras need me." Wild horses would not drag him away then, and many concerts did intervene.

Thus, everything seemed against his making a complete recovery. Although his old gay spirit once more prevailed, I felt behind that outward show a veiled touchiness that was new in him and betokened the weariness of the spirit.

The Promenade season opened on Saturday 19 June. Henry disliked this early start, always feeling he had no time for quiet preparatory study. Normally, when the Promenade Concerts opened on the first Saturday after Bank Holiday and the Royal Academy term ended with the orchestral concert early in July, Henry had a few weeks' quiet study before the preliminary rehearsals. But war, with its inexorable wickedness, made inexorable demands, and daylight lessened the peril from air attack for great gatherings of people such as those attending the Proms. Henry realized that it was wise to bring the concerts forward by nearly two months to gain daylight hours, but it grieved him that the war inevitably shattered tradition and his chance of quiet relaxation. He knew, however, that war was in this way making demands on him just as it did in such diverse ways in so many lives.

The opening concert on Saturday 19 June brought a packed house. Nearly all were young people, Henry observed, as he stood facing them to direct the singing of the National Anthem. His benign smile seemed to embrace the whole of this vast, youthful audience as one big family. Then he turned to direct Bax's *London Pageant* and so to the full concert; Heddle Nash was singing the lovely Handel aria "Love in her eyes sits playing", and Moura Lympany was the soloist in Saint-Saens's

Piano Concerto No. 2 in G minor. Henry was utterly tired of Beethoven's No. 5, although the London Philharmonic Orchestra were splendid and rose to it as though to a new work, but I know he hoped he would not have to direct it again for a long time. It had become so much a part of England's defiance—a theme rapped out each night on the radio and requested wherever an orchestra was available—that through constant repetition it sounded more like a slogan than music. From Dukas's *L'Apprenti Sorcier*, an epic lesson to all young would-be conductors and to many others of older standing, Henry extracted every ounce of its descriptive fun. He revelled in its gaiety and enjoyed it as much as the public every time he repeated it.

After the long programme I insisted on some rest. "Yes, Henry, you *are* going to stop in bed all day! It's Sunday." Telegrams, flowers and messages poured in and kept him from further study. On Monday the 21st, Basil Cameron came to share the concerts until 17 July, when the B.B.C. Symphony Orchestra and Sir Adrian Boult took over. That Monday Henry seemed glad to have got his rehearsal over in good time, in order to give Basil Cameron as long as possible for the new work by the American composer Walter Piston, a *Sinfonietta*. The concert included Brahms's *Tragic* overture, a Mozart aria "*L'Améro o costante*" (*Il Re Pastore*), sung by Noel Eadie, and the Mozart Pianoforte Concerto No. 4 in B flat, with Myra Hess as soloist. Then there was the Brahms Symphony No. 2 in D.

The Fates were kind to me that night. I decided not to go to the front of the hall, so that when Henry came off the platform I could be at hand to keep visitors at bay. Thus I did not witness the tragic happening. The Brahms symphony went its way, certainly a fine, broad 'Wood' performance save for the final movement. Listening, I knew something was wrong—not so strong a beat. To resounding applause he came off the platform, his body bent to the right. He was terribly hot and angry: "Damn silly," he exclaimed, "I've tried to keep upright, can't understand it—had to beat almost below the desk."

"Come and sit down," I urged, horribly aware what was wrong. "No, dear, I must bow, they're still applauding," Henry replied. And back on to the platform he went, still bent sideways, did his bow and acknowledged the orchestra in his customary manner. "Now home," I said, the moment he left the platform. I telephoned our doctor at once.

"A month in bed for you, Henry, my friend," was Lord Horder's decision in consultation with our doctor the following morning. The thought of a month in bed presented a picture slightly less grim than death to Henry. Although he had been carefully warned, he felt himself to be quite normal within twenty-four hours and persisted in questioning me as to the possibility of getting back to work without a fortnight at the most. It was a difficult time, for I knew Henry well enough to realize that if his doctors determined on a certain course, Henry would agree with them and possibly carry out to the letter all their instructions with seemingly cheerful resignation, but inside he would worry and fret so much as to undo all the good of the forced rest.

During the first few days it was suggested that he should take at least six months off duty. Greeted with a smile of acquiescence, it seemed to his doctors that their advice was gladly, almost warmly, accepted. Not a bit of it. He immediately told me he simply could not let the whole of the current season go by default. "If I do as suggested, I shall give up altogether. I couldn't approach next year, the jubilee year of the Promenade Concerts. I simply can't do that," he said. There was an inevitable compromise. Henry saw to it that others came round to his way of thinking. That was his way, an extraordinary, compelling 'direction' that brought his opponents round to his viewpoint while they were innocently under the impression that he was bowing to their decisions. He managed to cajole and persuade the doctors into allowing him to attend the Sunday afternoon Promenade Concert on 11 July. Freedom! Once out and about again, it would have been agonizing frustration for him to have delayed for long his return to the Promenade Concerts and the rostrum.

Basil Cameron shouldered alone the conducting of the whole four weeks of Henry's illness, a feat of endurance made possible only by his knowledge of the repertoire, combined with cultured musicianship and his determination to be of service to Henry. At first Henry made little comment either about his enforced rest or about the concerts, but as he gradually allowed despondency to give place to a certain irritability at being kept prisoner, he asked to have the wireless in his room.

"Ah," he often said as he listened, "you can only do what Basil is doing so wonderfully by long and varied experience. I owe him my gratitude."

I, too, was glad that it thus fell to Basil to direct the Rachmaninoff memorial concert on Friday 25 June, for I am sure that had the blow not fallen on the previous Monday, the emotional strain of the Chopin Funeral March and Rachmaninoff's Symphony No. 3 would have made Henry's illness worse.

A Sunday afternoon Promenade Concert—there was a departure from tradition! It was explained in a notice which appeared in the later prospectuses of the concerts:

"The Concert announced to take place on July 7 has been transferred to Sunday, July 11, at 2.30 p.m., owing to the Royal Albert Hall being required by H.M. Government for a meeting in honour of China on the occasion of the Sixth Anniversary of outbreak of the Sino-Japanese War. The programme will remain unchanged."

As I have said, Henry was allowed to drive over and take his place in our box, his first time out for seventeen days, with John Sebastian Bach to celebrate it. "Well, dear," said Henry, driving home through the park where he had rested for a while to feast on the lovely view from the Serpentine bridge towards Kensington Palace, "let's get the jubilee year behind us and then I shall be happy to become a regular concert-goer, there at the Proms every night, but not to conduct every night."

He also planned to teach singing regularly and wanted me to assist him. Well, man proposes, God disposes; but I know he would have liked a little more freedom from the hard grind imposed by war conditions. It was just one performance after another until the work seemed a dead end. These war years took their toll of all, from musicians to munition workers.

After the visit to the Albert Hall as a member of the audience, Henry had another quiet week, then returned to his beloved colleagues and his public. There was no fuss, and certainly no fear. Just a brisk "Now let's get on with the job." He returned to work with a set purpose once more to *will* the impossible, as had happened with the Hull Orchestra, but this time it was to subdue and control his own health against all odds and at the age of seventy-four. For the rest of the season he showed all his old serenity and nothing was lost musically.

The old fire returned, glowing throughout the remaining thirty concerts.

The B.B.C. suggested that he should speak on the last night, but I feared the strain would be too great. He always said that speaking in public made him nervous and kept him awake for nights on end. We finally decided to record the speech and play it back in the Albert Hall. This device came off wonderfully well and he was received with jubilation by the vast family of friends when he made his reappearance on the platform. I think it was taken for granted that he had actually spoken to them from a microphone in his retiring-room.

"A holiday for you now, my dear Henry," I said. "Where shall it be?"

"Let's go where I can paint and we can be quietly together," he replied.

So we set off by road to Beaumaris on 1 September, Lord Horder coming over to see us off at eight o'clock in the morning. How Henry revelled in that journey, like a schoolboy travelling for the first time! The picnic lunch by the wayside, the scenery, the freedom, all delighted him, and he was a new man on arrival at Beaumaris, where he was thrilled with the enchanting view over the Menai Straits from our window. "I can paint here," he exclaimed—and at once began to assemble easel, paint-box, brushes, turps., and all the paraphernalia inseparable from oil-painting. Although he dabbled from day to day, his sketches did not please him and most of them were destroyed. But rest he certainly did in the quiet and peace of a lovely little spot in the Islands.

The last little canvas Henry painted is like a water-colour in texture, a lovely conception of light colour and mistiness over the straits, looking to the Welsh hills on the mainland.

I am glad he finished his painting like that, quiet and beautiful in thought, with no sense of urgency.

The little picture remains for me a symbol of sixteen days resplendent with memories of a happy and released Henry, freed almost against his will from the other Henry, the slave of music. I see in those serene days a Henry friendly and approachable to strangers, a Henry interested in local affairs.

Sixteen days off duty, however, made the urge for music too insistent to be denied, so home we drove to a miscellany of activities in London culminating in the beloved students' rehearsals at the Royal Academy which began again on 28 September. The return to London also brought back to his memory the tragic death of his old friend B. J. Dale, late warden of the Royal Academy of Music, who had died suddenly in the Albert Hall after a rehearsal. For some time after this sad event Henry could not get it out of his head and talked constantly of the many Dale compositions which should have had hearings. "Before the Paling of the Stars" for chorus and orchestra was a favourite, and "The Flowing Tide" is a lovely work for full orchestra. It was the excitement of the coming first performance of "The Flowing Tide" which undoubtedly caused the composer's sudden passing.

A memorial service to Mr. Dale was the first appointment noted in Henry's diary on returning from Beaumaris. But Henry did not attend, reminding me most emphatically that he disagreed with this kind of 'arranged' farewell. Later on, when some insisted on such a service as the right course after Henry's own death, the memory of what he had said strengthened my resolve to carry out his wishes—that those mindful of him should attend the service of farewell in the presence of the remains of a staunch colleague and a loved friend.

During 1943, Henry planned to institute a recognized and

permanent arrangement with the L.C.C. to allow children of up to fifteen years of age to attend the Promenade Concert rehearsals free of charge. He was prompted and encouraged to do this by the response of some of the teachers who had been bringing hundreds of London school-children to the rehearsals since 1941. It was a happy arrangement, and Henry's only major stipulation was that the children should be kept out of the first blocks of seats and as far as conveniently possible from the orchestra. He did not like people to be within verbal hearing during rehearsals, feeling it was improper that any-one should overhear what a conductor said to his orchestra, especially if he had to be rather sharper than usual. He dis-agreed, too, with afternoon rehearsals for an evening concert, especially for the longer programmes of the Promenade Concerts. He desired worthy preparation for a concert which the public pays to hear. He was also much opposed to after-noon rehearsals for singers, for the human voice requires much more care than any other instrument, and it may tire the delicate vocal cords to perform in the evening so soon after an afternoon rehearsal.

CHAPTER 9

Promenade Jubilee

TOWARDS THE END of 1943 Henry made a new version of his
famous Purcell-Wood *Trumpet Voluntary*. He found this little
work often requested, frequently for performances in provincial concert halls where there was no organ available or,
if there were an organ, one usually tuned to the old high
pitch. So he scored the voluntary for full orchestra, and Messrs.
Chappell & Co. published the work. The controversy regarding the composer—Purcell or Jeremiah Clarke—amused Henry
greatly, for it was actually he who started the argument afresh.
It occurred to him that if he made a version for full orchestra,
the publisher might avoid the obligation of sharing the royalties with the owners of the original organ piece, arranged by
Dr. Sparkes, if it was published as a work by Jeremiah Clarke.
The idea was dropped for various reasons, but it stirred anew
the old dispute over the identity of the original composer.
Henry was personally quite convinced that the lovely little
trumpet piece was the work of Purcell, and his two versions
are in the name of Purcell-Wood.

On 26 October Henry acceded to Eliot Seabrook's very
earnest invitation to open an exhibition of the London Group
of artists at Burlington House. "Art, painting? Oh, yes," he
had said with eagerness when the topic was first raised. Then,
as the significance of the engagement dawned on him, his
enthusiasm rapidly waned: "Speech? Mmmm!" Another
thought struck him. "The date is bad. It is my day for the
Royal Academy Students' Orchestra." And at that, if he could
have backed out he would have done.

Finally he decided: "I won't lose the whole afternoon as I can get the Burlington House ceremony over by 1 p.m. and Ernest Reed will take an hour of my rehearsal for me, I know." And from the picture exhibition, he sped back home to a light lunch, changed, and hurried on to the real joy of his musical life—the students' orchestra.

Henry looked forward to the year 1944 with a certain amount of concern. It was evident he would be called upon to attend many functions and would have to make those dreaded public speeches. In October 1943 a movement emanated from Broadcasting House to establish in some tangible way the jubilee of the Promenade Concerts in 1944 and at the same time commemorate Henry's seventy-fifth birthday in March the same year. It was also hoped that the highest official recognition would be conferred upon him at this time. That all this did not bear full fruit was no fault of Henry's friends inside Broadcasting House, whose aims were frustrated in no little degree by some academic colleagues. But one thing, at about this time, encouraged and delighted him amid the non-musical anxieties of the future arrangements—it was a meeting on 16 December 1943, to discuss the 1944 Proms. "It looks as though they are really going to get things well in advance, thank goodness," Henry said. The comfortable thought that plenty of time was being given to preparation made a short rest in the country over Christmas all the happier.

And then the year 1944 began. Invitations to lunches, dinners and other functions began pouring in in such numbers that it was impossible to accept them all. When he could, Henry preferred to have his friends about him at a quiet lunch in his own home, and it was a joy when such a dear friend as Granville Bantock, among others, came over.

Then began a series of committee meetings of various kinds and, of course, discussions on programmes for the jubilee Promenade Concerts. I recall a luncheon which Lord Camrose gave in February to discuss the jubilee concert which the *Daily Telegraph* would sponsor, and gatherings with many close friends—Julia Neilson, Baroness de Bush, Mrs. Saleeby, Zelie de Lursan, Lady Ross and Billy and Marion Squire—not directly connected with the working end of music. But these 'off duty' lunches gave Henry the pleasure of a youngster out for the first time.

All through January and into February the intensive planning went ahead, until one day brought the remark: "What about some music?"

However, he still had his R.A.M. rehearsals every Tuesday and he would have loved just to teach those young people every day. Then, on 20 February, the tenth anniversary of Elgar's death, Henry gave a fine rendering of the First Symphony in a special 'Elgar' broadcast from the B.B.C. studio at Bedford. Up to the last moment it had been hoped that the Royal Albert Hall would be available for the *Daily Telegraph's* tribute concert for Henry's seventy-fifth birthday on 3 March. But damage caused by enemy action was taking longer to repair than anticipated and so it was postponed until the 25th. So often all my efforts to keep exhausting events spaced out at fairly wide intervals in order to give Henry a chance for plenty of rest in between were frustrated by unforeseen difficulties of this kind.

On 2 March the Performing Right Society gave a luncheon at Grosvenor House in Henry's honour and presented him the same day with a beautifully illuminated album containing hundreds of autographs of musicians the world over. The presentation was made in Duke's Hall at the Royal

Academy. It was a wonderful collection of names, some with delightfully kind messages, others recalling concertos or arias performed under Henry's direction. It was a moving moment for Henry when Dr. Vaughan Williams made the presentation, and Leslie Boosey, on behalf of the society, handed Henry a cheque for one thousand guineas as a jubilee gift. The money went, at Henry's wish, into his Jubilee Fund which was to be devoted to music students or to building a concert hall to replace the lost Queen's Hall. In his reply Henry spoke well, always with notes, but with freedom and a full-hearted pleasure in the honours showered upon him. The most touching memory of this day—and he often spoke of it with deep gratitude—was the arrangement made by the Performing Right Society for the wonderful album to be exhibited in the Duke's Hall. Many musicians had travelled from all over Britain for the presentation, and I particularly remember Henry's only regret being that the timetable arrangements did not permit his turning the gathering into a large informal party, so that he could talk with all the musicians who had paid him such a signal tribute. Dear Frank Mullings, for instance, came up from Manchester by a very early train. Never before had such a concourse of professional musicians joined forces to honour one of themselves. Afterwards, as Henry turned over the pages of the album—turning them slowly with that light, almost reverent, touch peculiar to him when reading a piece of music script or a book— he said: "We must have a gathering together of all those friends who have signed this book as soon as all this jubilee business is over. I *should* like to meet them all without fuss or hurry."

Then we had to travel down to Manchester again and I recall many meetings there with Marie and Oscar Pulvermacher. (It was Oscar Pulvermacher who, while editing the *Daily Telegraph* in Manchester, first suggested the *Daily Telegraph* birthday tribute.) Then back to London again, and throughout all the air warfare there I only once saw it openly affect Henry. That was on 14 March, when there was a pretty wretched noise right over us.

One event of this year came as a very real surprise to Henry. He was invited to a luncheon at the Savage Club without being given the slightest warning of what was afoot. So far as he knew, it was one of the regular house-luncheons, at which distinguished fellow-Savages were sometimes entertained, presided over on this occasion by Stanley Rubinstein. The invitation caused Henry some concern, for he was still carefully advised by his doctors to go slow and had been obliged to cancel engagements, but, thinking he would be able just to say a few words of thanks for the lunch, he set off for the Savage Club against his doctor's orders. At the club, however, he was dumbfounded by the display of affection, and told me afterwards that when he was presented with an album containing contributions from many famous Savages, with drawings, paintings, etc., he felt completely speechless with surprise. Henry, who normally was never demonstrative, was so moved that he was thrown off his balance that day. This volume was scanned daily. "A picture gallery", he would say, and: "How generous they are in speaking of my music." I feel certain that Henry would like this wonderful tribute to find a permanent home with his brother Savages, and at the appropriate time I shall ask of them this curatorship. He had been made an honorary life member some years previously, and often, when looking through that marvellous book, he expressed the hope that "once this jubilee business is over, I mean to know more of my brother Savages".

A few days' rest saw the natural colour returning to his cheeks, which had assumed a grey, drawn look associated with his illness. He returned to London refreshed and fit for the Musicians' Benevolent Fund luncheon on 24 March, now to be followed by the postponed *Daily Telegraph* birthday concert on 25 March.

It was a representative meeting of musicians which that indefatigable secretary, Frank Thistleton, had gathered together at the Savoy and over which the chairman, Frank Howes, presided. Thank goodness, a happy atmosphere prevailed. Henry was able to speak with pleasure and ease. He found himself the possessor of yet another album, signed by all present and containing as well the original verses which John Masefield had written for the occasion. Later Henry also received a contribution of £300 for his Jubilee Fund.

One birthday letter gave Henry almost tearful pleasure. It was from John Masefield:

"Dear Sir Henry Wood,

"The poets must all be hurrying to the post with letters of gladness and congratulations to you, and many of them will be older, and few of them can have so long an indebtedness to you, for hours upon hours of delight. For those hours, and the long indebtedness, let me now try to thank you, as the entire nation tried to thank you, with the most grateful thoughts and gladness that you have lived to see England the most musical among the lands of the world. May your birthday be glad, and may you for many years bring the delight of music to this war-shaken planet.

"With all thanks and praise,

"John Masefield."

This tribute evoked another example of Henry's great modesty. Deeply touched by the Poet Laureate's words, Henry looked at the letter wonderingly, and exclaimed:

"Who would have thought he knew me?"

On 1 June the Royal Academy of Music gave an informal lunch at the Academy, followed by a lovely concert from the Griller String Quartet and Clifford Curzon. Henry was warmly appreciative, thanking the (then) principal, Sir Stanley Marchant, and rolling off a jolly speech. He was so completely at home in the Duke's Hall. The Griller Quartet is well known, but what is perhaps not quite so well known is that the four players—Sidney Griller, Jack O'Brien, Philip Burton and Colin Hampton—started together well over a quarter of a century ago. All four were students of the Royal Academy. Henry was thrilled with their playing, and defied anyone to find a finer chamber music ensemble. And Clifford Curzon too. "What a student he had been and now what an artist!" as Henry said. It was a grand day, enjoyable and free from fuss. On visits to the Royal Academy Henry always looked for Gurney Parrott, secretary of the R.A.M. Henry loved to slip into Parrott's room for a cup of tea and quiet gossip, either during the interval of his rehearsal or before leaving. It was a much treasured friendship.

A B.B.C. luncheon at Claridge's on 5 June found Henry in quite a gay mood. Another cheque for one thousand guineas was presented to him which, as with other large sums, he passed on for his Jubilee Fund. Henry, in his speech of thanks, discussed his views on the future of the Promenade Concerts in a way that illustrated his wonderful spirit of generosity and freedom from rancour.

In the unhappy, frustrating negotiations of 1939 and 1940, while waiting for the B.B.C. to come to a conclusion as to whether or not to run the 1940 season of Promenade Concerts, Henry had often exclaimed: "I won't have anything more to do with the B.B.C." He well remembered that time as he prepared his speech of thanks for the festive luncheon and all the good wishes which the B.B.C. showered upon him, and clearly showed that he bore no malice. On the contrary, he bestowed upon them another gift, that of his name, when he declared:

"When my dear old friend and manager, Robert Newman, died in 1926, Chappells decided not to proceed with the 1927 season of Promenade Concerts after having been responsible for them for eleven years—from 1915 to be precise. It at first looked somewhat doubtful whether the 1927 season could in fact mature, for although some would-be managements had approached me, none I felt wholly at one with me in a policy which had proved successful beyond all dreams—a policy of gradual education through well-planned entertainment in the realm of serious music.

"The B.B.C. then proposed taking over the responsibility of continuing the Promenade Concerts, and from the outset of negotiations, which were of a purely political nature since I required nothing but that the Promenade Concerts should go on, arrangements were made that ensured this. Out of these negotiations, the most difficult problem to solve appeared to rest in the title of my orchestra."

Henry then recalled that the title "The New Queen's Hall Orchestra" was held by Messrs. Chappells, who were unwilling to let the B.B.C. use it. "Eventually we hit upon 'Sir Henry Wood and his Symphony Orchestra'—a dreadful title but it served the purpose of continuity in the mind of the public," he declared, adding:

"With this new title and many of my old players round me, I directed my first orchestral broadcast, eighteen years ago on 20 January 1927, when the B.B.C. was just learning to toddle at four years old. But the title business underwent another change three years later when in 1930 it was merged into the B.B.C. Symphony Orchestra and which it remains today; so that in no small measure I feel somewhat the father of serious orchestral broadcasting. . . . I shall always look back with satisfaction on the decision of 1926, and to the first season under the direction of the B.B.C. in 1927, when new life was infused into these concerts. In fact they were saved and much else musically, for there can be no doubt that the wide field open to wireless listeners clinched the steady, up-growing sense of serious music in our country. It was indeed a decision expounding an axiom I endorse—the greatest good to the greatest number.

"And here we are, close upon our jubilee season. The Corporation has marked the occasion with uncommon good-will and a friendliness that touches me, and of which I am fully conscious, knowing as I do that by their so intimate and whole-hearted co-operation the ultimate success of the Jubilee Fund is assured, and that out of it will rise a concert hall worthy of London, the empire's heart, and of our now unchallenged right as the centre of all that is best in music. Lord Horder, as chairman of the Jubilee Fund committee, and the members of his committee are all very busy men, and I realize, and am deeply conscious of, the honour they do me in serving on this committee in the ultimate interests of music—a concert hall to hold four thousand comfortably seated, acoustically perfect, and in a situation favourable to simple and easy journeys for Greater Londoners and those in the provinces.

"It is my desire to perpetuate my life's work for the good of the people, and to secure that my Promenade Concerts are carried on after my retirement. The B.B.C. is surely now the guardian of the people's music, and my Promenade Concerts have always been the people's concerts. I have therefore decided to invite the B.B.C. to become curator, and to accept the right to continue to present the Henry Wood Promenade Concerts annually for so long as they care to carry them on, and I am happy to think that the B.B.C. have accepted that right in the spirit in which it is offered. It would be a sad day, not only for me but, in my view, for the people and for music if the B.B.C. ever decided to substitute some other concerts for the Henry Wood Promenade Concerts. It is not easy to see what the conditions for music may be in years to come, or what the private impresario of the future may be like, and so I hope with all my heart that the B.B.C. will carry on my Promenade Concerts as a permanent annual institution, for the good of the people for all time."

Not all the plans and hopes touched on in that speech have come to pass. Queen's Hall has not been rebuilt, and the Royal Festival Hall has risen—so that there now seems no prospect of Henry's vision of a fine concert hall, built from the Jubilee Fund contributions, ever being fulfilled.

CHAPTER 10

Henry Stricken

THE JUBILEE SEASON of the Promenade Concerts opened at
the Royal Albert Hall on 10 June 1944 amid great rejoicings.
The concerts continued the following evenings to packed and
overflowing audiences in spite of Hitler's furies. But before
the end of the month we were deprived of the Albert Hall by
authorities anxious about what would happen if one of the
fearful flying bombs landed on the packed building. This was
the period when the first of Hitler's 'secret weapons' were
being directed against London in an effort to crumple British
morale and the Home Secretary, Herbert Morrison, had drawn
up plans to evacuate 1,000,000 Londoners if the threat became
too pressing. Clearly the carnage would have been terrible if
one of the buzz-bombs had exploded amongst the packed
thousands during one of the concerts, so the heartrending
decision was taken to close the public concerts and continue
the season over the radio.

Thus we left the London Philharmonic Orchestra in London
and followed the B.B.C. Symphony Orchestra to its then wartime headquarters in Bedford. Never shall I forget the demonstration of affection and appreciation which met Henry when
the orchestra, not too happy in its provincial quarters, saw
him. It was as if they had missed him more than usual—a rare
demonstration which touched Henry very deeply.

After Henry had directed a wonderful performance of 'En
Saga', Paul Beard cried, literally, with tears of joy and musical
satisfaction. He jumped up and greeted Henry with both hands
outstretched:

"Thank you, Sir Henry, that is living again—that is what musicians need."

Dear Paul came to Henry's room where he was changing after the broadcast and shyly almost apologized for his outburst in the hall of Bedford School where the concert was held. "Oh, you don't know how wonderful it has been tonight after months of studio routine," he said.

That was on Saturday 8 July. For the following two weeks the orchestra gave Henry all he asked of them. Then gradually the 'studio routine', the insidious influences of war, evacuation, frustration and difficult living conditions began to assert themselves upon the players once more.

Henry at this time became more insistent than ever that I never left his side. I remember only too well one day in this month of July when I had to go up to London because a flying bomb had shattered the windows of our London home. I always liked Henry to rest in bed whenever he had a chance because of the strain of this jubilee year, so I suggested that he should remain in bed until I returned, which would be by the first possible train after lunch. He had already been working on scores for the Friday Prom broadcast, and so I said: "Why not quietly read a book?" But no. The scores for the morrow had to be left on his bed-table. When I returned, I was hailed as though I had been away for months instead of a few hours. And then he said eagerly:

"Look, darling, I have worked right through the Beethoven Seventh, and I've found this—and this—that didn't come off last time I did it. I *am* looking forward to the rehearsal."

All that evening he would not let go my hand. "Oh, it was such a long morning," he sighed, "and I was so worried about your being in London without me. I listened to the news, and what a relief it was when no report of more 'doodles' came through. Don't leave me alone again, we mustn't be away from each other."

We had dinner at the Bridge Hotel and Mr. Thompson, B.B.C. concert manager, joined us at my suggestion to discuss plans for the following week, for all programmes were subject to revision while the Proms continued over the air from Bedford.

Henry was quite cross. He told me afterwards he did not want anyone else to share an evening 'together again' (I had been absent just five hours). Constant Lambert came through the lounge later on, after Mr. Thompson had left, and, spotting us, walked over to introduce—at her request presumably —Lady Keynes who had been attending a ballet music broadcast. This, too, made Henry restless, and when I invited them to join us in a drink he murmured:

"But, darling, I don't want other people to intrude on this evening."

It was a curious mood, though I know that of course he had been under a considerable strain while I was in London, and this anxiety overlaid his worry and disappointment over the mood of the orchestra.

The studio tedium had again taken hold of the orchestra— but Henry just could not press his wishes as he would have done under normal conditions; he had seen for himself the anxieties they suffered severally and felt a compassionate desire to let them understand his solicitude without the emotion of voicing it. But it didn't work that way, and just before my hurried visit to London an incident occurred that caused Henry considerable fret—the very thing we had tried so hard to avoid. Henry's doctor had said:

"Let him do anything so long as he is happy, but at all costs avoid the emotional strain of anger, for that would be perilous with his health as it is."

The occasion was a Bach rehearsal—and Henry's Bach was apparently a stranger to many of the players. Unlike some conductors he never treated Bach with that carefree "let-the-music-speak-for-itself" attitude. No morning of lax attention for him; no sewing-machine rhythm. But it became plain in the first five minutes of rehearsal that few minds were really concentrating on the all-important beat from the rostrum. Watching, I became alarmed. The players, had they watched, would have seen his eye, which was just as much a part of his compelling direction as the stick and left hand request.

The response was ragged; the players seemed to have no conception of what Henry was asking of them. Suddenly he stopped and, leaning over his stand, said loudly and crossly:

"Gentlemen, I know it is only Bach, Johann Sebastian Bach. But you don't know Bach. Can you see my beat?"

"Yes," came the reply.

"Can you understand my beat?"

"Yes."

"Well, you are not looking. *You are not looking.* Now we shall have to go through that movement again."

How angry he was perhaps I alone knew, for he never ranted at the players. But I saw the anguish and frustration in his eye. When we were back in our room at the hotel, he said:

"Darling Jessie, to think I receive this answer to my years of work for dear John Sebastian Bach, and an established orchestra of musicians cannot ride above their tedium to meet a living request."

I implored him not to direct the broadcast that night.

"What," he said. "You, of all people, ask me to stand aside and let John Sebastian Bach down? Never!"

And so he directed the broadcast, and the orchestra, I must

say, responded with some show of interest if not with a particularly deep understanding of the master.

Later I urged him to have supper sent up to our rooms but he said he wanted to go down and forget the day.

28 July saw us down to breakfast. He looked tired but maintained a tranquil mood—although not the quiet, confident tranquillity I wished for—and there was a glint of determination in his eyes. He met the orchestra cheerfully that morning, with his usual business-like approach, making no reference to the miserable Bach episode.

The aria, "Ah Perfido", with Joan Hammond, received quick attention, and then Henry told them:

"We must go through this again. You do not know how to accompany recitative. This is a recitative; just watch my beat. You watch—watch my beat."

Then came Maurice Cole in a Mozart concerto, badly accompanied. Henry stopped them several times, remarking:

"Oh, yes. I know *you* know this concerto, ladies and gentlemen, and so does Mr. Cole. So do I. But this artist is here to rehearse it, so please give it your attention."

To my surprise, although he had time and to spare, Henry merely touched up certain points in the symphony, and then said in his customary manner: "Good morning, gentlemen." The rehearsal was over. Henry was devoted to Paul Beard, and knew he had the complete confidence, even affection, of this great leader, and so no reflection rests upon him here— nor for that matter on any musician of the orchestra. After all, this unhappy episode was just, as was so much else, force of circumstances created by the war—and Henry thought no more of it.

On the way to the hotel I said: "Why did you not go through No. 7 after having put so much time and thought into it?"—for it was the Beethoven on which he had worked so hard during my visit to London.

"What?" he exploded. "Rehearse a repertoire piece with them in their present mood? No, my dear. But *I shall make them play it to-night.*"

I was terribly anxious. He had that tense look when his very blue eyes seemed to take on a steely colour, always a mark of deep inner thought and extreme tension. All through lunch he was very grave, suffering, I know, in sorrow rather than anger. Repeatedly he said he could not understand professional musicians so losing respect for their work. I did my best to soothe him, but each time he said:

"Never mind, I'll make 'em play to-night."

He rested during the afternoon, if one can call lying on his bed and thinking 'resting'. He could not and would not drop the subject of the orchestra.

"I cannot understand those players. They are no longer musicians. Just like civil servants," he exclaimed.

I thought that if I left him alone he might drop the topic. But within five minutes of my leaving the room he sent for me. "Darling Jessie, don't leave me," he said. So I sat there beside him, and finally he dropped off to sleep and rested quietly for an hour at last.

Despite his anguish over the music, Henry sympathized wholeheartedly with the problems brought on by the war which lay behind the trouble. These orchestral musicians, men and women, had been uprooted and packed off to the homes of strangers in Bristol, Evesham, and finally Bedford. In common with millions of people they suffered discomforts, grievances and anxieties about their children, their parents, or husbands or wives—all separated and frustrated, sometimes in danger.

This had now been going on for a full five years—an anxious, cheerless life in billets. It is understandable that the utter weariness that was beginning to infect such a great proportion of the British people at this time, men and women just waiting for the war to end, spread to these musicians as well and the personnel was always on the move. The 'call-up' moved player after player.

From their billets they went to rehearsals, which offered an opportunity to meet their fellow players and air this or that spot of bother one with the other—clothing, food, shopping, news of a sudden death or illness occupied their individual minds instead of that fusion of ninety egos into a single, united orchestra. Dear old Henry realized their dull, miserable existence and all their human emotions, but he just could not understand the gradual lapsing back into unmusical thought in two short weeks after that unforgettable demonstration on his arrival in Bedford. But there it was—the environment was too strong. Much as they appreciated Henry's coming to Bedford, their real lives for the time being consisted of the same old faces, the same scrounge for a smile from the butcher, the baker, the greengrocer, the milkman—everything. Such daily tasks so easily led to slipshod despair and dulled enthusiasm.

That night there was about Henry a strange want of his usual calm. For no reason that I could detect, the dressing was hurried. He literally ran down the steps from our hotel and hastened me over the bridge as though we were late. In fact there was a full half hour to spare. The little hall was packed with an invited audience and as usual I was to sit just where he could see me: it was his invariable request. This was a simple matter to manage at the Bedford concerts; it was more difficult at public concerts elsewhere. All the same he had to know just where I was sitting when I went into the auditorium—for in the last years I often remained behind in the wings in case an emergency arose. When he came on to the platform he would always bow to my place first; and then, just before raising his baton for the opening work, he would turn right round and look at me and pass a silent greeting. I thank God for the happiness my presence always brought him.

When the red light—indicating that we were on the air— appeared that evening of 28 July 1944, he went up to the rostrum, a contraption large enough to house four or five conductors, and took up his stick. Then he turned to where I was sitting, away on his left, and instead of his usual smile of satisfaction and poised assurance, he turned a steely eye on me and distinctly said "Now!" before turning to the orchestra. I cannot describe what clutched my heart, for as his first beat went down I felt Henry was making music as only he knew how, but was making music for the last time.

He set out to do just what he had planned. He looked round his orchestra, as always. But again I noticed, as he looked to his left to make sure all the players there were ready, the same cold steely-blue eye in place of that kindly "now we are about to enjoy ourselves" glance. Cold fear gripped me. Something told me that this was the trial which would break even his indomitable spirit. Here was a man who had given his life to a cause and he was willing to surrender his stay on earth to it. To make those players, some of them indolent and inattentive, wake up to become the musicians they really were, he gave more strength of will than he could at that time afford. And I watched.

Beethoven's Seventh Symphony went over the air and into the homes of Britain (I am told, as never before) with every joyous note; and every player was brought to the call of that insistent eye and beat. Indeed, though full of fear, I knew I was listening to this work as never before heard. It was joyous, electric Beethoven.

Henry acknowledged the reception from both orchestra and audience with his usual calm sweet smile and quiet dignity. There was no haste, nothing but a cheery nod here and a word there as we went to our car. (I always insisted on the car home or a change in the hall after a performance on account of his wet clothes.) As soon as we were alone, he gave me his customary embrace with: "Thank you, darling. I made 'em play, didn't I?" He had the cheeky, even youthful, smile with a twinkle in his eyes. But his face was very tired and drawn.

After he had changed his clothing I begged him to get right into bed.

"No, I may look tired, but it was only that extra urge to make the Beethoven Seventh, without rehearsal, sound as none of us had ever imagined it! Come on, darling Jessie, let's have supper."

Supper! Food refused to pass my throat, and although Henry had quite a good meal I shall always believe that he made himself eat to try to allay the fear he knew was in my heart. My fear had not been expressed, but we knew each other so well. He noticed that I realized all was not well with him in spite of his jaunty manner and his determination to have a whisky and soda instead of the usual gentle glass of wine.

To bed. He was so cold and getting so grey and yellow. But he slept for a few hours, while I listened to his heavy breathing, to his muffled chatter and the grinding of his teeth. About one in the morning he suddenly awoke and said he was very cold and felt sick. Cold as ice, and sick, he was. And then, almost before I could get a fresh hot-water bottle, another of those dreaded shiverings, another rigor, set in. I was back again to that dreadful hour of 1943. I roused all available help and called a doctor; a stranger, of course, as there was no time to get anyone who knew him well. Later I telephoned Lord Horder and he hurried from Scotland, reaching us on the Monday.

At the time there was a strange 'bug' causing anxiety among American troops in this country, and although I persisted that Henry always assumed a yellow, jaundiced look round his eyes and ears when he was upset, the local doctor insisted on taking certain blood tests and blood counts. Henry kept saying in that resonant slow speech of his:

"What's all this? What is it all *for*?"

Of course, no 'bug' could be detected.

When Lord Horder came Henry had rallied, and, although his temperature had been 104 the day before, he appeared on Monday to be recovering and regaining a more normal colour. He talked with Lord Horder and pleaded for long drinks of iced water. It looked as if I had acted needlessly in calling Lord Horder from his holiday. On Tuesday 1 August Henry really was almost normal. He wanted to know who was conducting, what was in the programme and so on.

But he kept asking for fruit and liquids. I went all over Bedford trying to find grapes, peaches or oranges, but in wartime it was like asking for gold. Henry Wood was not a regular customer there. Dear Elsie Newmarch, an old friend, then sent some frequently from London, and herself came armed with everything she felt he might like.

CHAPTER 11

Last Hours

NURSES CAME TO take over some of the constant care Henry needed, but no one gave him more willing and dear help than a Sister Murch. I simply don't know what I should have done without her help and advice. She was living in the hotel looking after the proprietress, who had been seriously ill. She would take sheets, nightshirts and handkerchiefs along and wash them out herself. More, she gave me a moral support which no one else afforded.

After the first two days of his illness Henry refused to take anything except water and iced milk. On the Thursday I went down for some food to find Jessie Hinchliffe, the violinist, and Walter Legge there. Jessie told me that after Henry's Beethoven Seventh the orchestra was completely exhausted. He had demanded so much; that insistent eye and stern, firm beat defied them all, daring even a single eye to leave the baton. The whole orchestra sent messages and asked for news, and for that he was grateful. Dear Solomon sent up a bottle of champagne which, alas, Henry could not drink. But he was so pleased, just nodding his head in approval.

Another delightful gesture which gave Henry much pleasure came from the Princess Royal. When Henry's illness was first made known, she sent him a charming letter and a bottle of barley sugar.

I could not help being struck by the part Beethoven's Seventh had played in taking so much of Henry's strength. As I have said earlier, it was after an exhausting performance of No. 7 when staying in Hertfordshire, conducting right through, that Henry suffered his seizure in 1943. And now, once more, it was No. 7, that most tiring of works to direct at the best of times, which preceded Henry's last illness.

On Friday 4 August there was a relapse and another terrible rigor. Yet he was seemingly little the worse afterwards except that he would take no nourishment. He wanted to leave the hotel, to get home if possible, but it was inadvisable to take him to our London home, because of the flying bombs and the noisy flights overhead. But although I ranged the whole Stevenage-Bedford district, no nursing home had room.

By 7 August Henry was so much better that a ray of real hope arose within me. He even tried some champagne—a quarter bottle, which Mr. Nicolls sent at my special request, was opened, for Henry would not allow the 'waste' of opening dear Solomon's gift. He was quite awake for long hours, showing a lively interest in the broadcasts of the Prom programmes and asking to hear Thalben Ball play the Handel No. 4 Organ Concerto which Henry had recently scored.

10 August was a day which as long as I live will stand for the truth that Henry's music was his whole life. He knew that on that day, fifty years before, he had opened the Proms at Queen's Hall. He was feverishly excited, flushed, and a little impishly determined to do as he wished. It was eventually agreed that he ought not to have a wireless in his room. So he asked me to listen in another room and tell him all about his newly orchestrated concerto and all the other items on the fiftieth anniversary programme. In this way he would be comforted and quite happy.

Henry had sent a message to his friends, the musical public, which Stuart Hibberd read over the air. Lord Horder made an appeal on "this great jubilee day" for donations to the Jubilee Fund (of which he was chairman) to further Henry's dream of building a new concert hall in London. Thalben Ball made a fine transmission over the air of Henry's scoring—an undoubted success—and so I went back to his bedside to relate it all. He listened, propped up with many pillows, and with that dear kind smile, so pleased that the jubilee day had been a great success in spite of his absence and Hitler's noises.

"That's over, dear Jessie. Dear Jessie, I'm so tired, I want to lie down."

As I finished describing that broadcast he turned on his side, saying:

"Fifty years! Fifty years!"

I felt within me that awful gripping fear afresh. I knew his tremendous will had now bowed to bodily fatigue. He was going to give in, but he had held on to live through his jubilee anniversary day.

On 14 August Dr. Skeggs and Dr. Calthrop came, and, in the hope we could yet do something more than sit and watch, helped to remove Henry to Hitchin Hospital.

"Why, why all this, dear Jessie? And why all those people?" he asked as he was lifted into the ambulance, around which a crowd collected.

There was nowhere for me to stay, so I went to Dr. Skeggs at Stevenage, a few minutes' drive away. On 17 August I was at the hospital from 8 a.m. until I was turned out by our night nurse. Henry had been his usual calm, dear self all day, holding my hand closely although he was very ill. On 18 August I was with him all day, and Lord Horder came to see him.

Dr. Skeggs and I were called very early in the morning of the 19th by our nurses. Henry almost sat up as I entered his room. "I telephoned and asked for you," he said.

In those last hours the panorama of our wonderful years passed and repassed before me.

And at 1.22 p.m. Henry Wood passed on.

CHAPTER 12

In Memoriam

DURING THE PLANNING for the 1944 jubilee, when it was hoped to commemorate in a lasting way both the half century of the Promenade Concerts and Henry's seventy-fifth birthday, a committee was formed with Lord Horder as chairman.

Some mention in passing of the aims and objects of this committee has already been made. The idea of collecting funds for a concert hall was not the first suggestion, however.

Henry's first choice was a students' scheme, whereby quarters would be provided where they could practise without fear of interference. The accommodation was to include, if funds ran to it, a hostel where the students could live comfortably while pursuing their studies in London.

I remember how Henry telephoned Edwin Evans, then music critic of the *Daily Telegraph* and an old friend, asking him to come and discuss the students' scheme with him; and the resulting notes were sent to Lord Horder. However, there were many difficulties which appeared to prevent the completion of this project, and, with Queen's Hall gone, Henry saw the immediate necessity for a concert hall helpful to symphonic music. After the rejection of the students' scheme, Henry went forward with all enthusiasm for the concert hall and sent his suggestion for a suitable site, together with a rough sketch of its possibilities, to the committee. The site— Park Square, Regent's Park—was in the right area, not far from the blitzed Queen's Hall, and, though it adjoined Marylebone Road, entrances could have been set on the east and west, thus avoiding any intrusion upon the main road traffic. The square is large enough to house a dignified concert hall and music centre while preserving the trees and general quiet beauty of this little attachment, which is really part of Regent's Park. Henry saw in this site London's great opportunity to build a concert hall worthy of our capital, competing favourably with the beautiful houses of music on the Continent and in America. On 8 June 1944 King George VI invested Henry with the Order of the Companions of Honour. The King asked him how his Jubilee Fund was going, and expressed the hope that Queen's Hall might be rebuilt or a new concert hall erected in Park Square.

Henry's dream of giving back to music the tribute the public wanted to give him during the jubilee celebrations did not mature before he died. And so it lingers on, with little prospect of showing the love people had for him—demonstrated in contributions from shillings to pounds.

Not only were there large contributions from, among others, the B.B.C., the Gramophone Company, and the Performing Right Society, which each presented Henry with a cheque for 1,000 guineas—allocated by him to his Jubilee Concert Hall—as well as the Musicians' Benevolent Fund, but the great Albert Hall birthday concert in 1944, sponsored by the *Daily Telegraph* and attended by the Queen and the two Princesses (now the Queen Mother, the present Queen and Princess Margaret), raised several thousands of pounds for the jubilee tribute. The programme, with the amalgamated London Symphony Orchestra, B.B.C. Symphony Orchestra, and London Philharmonic Orchestra directed in turn by Henry, Sir Adrian Boult, Basil Cameron and Dr. Malcolm Sargent, with Solomon, was:

Overture, *The Flying Dutchman* . . .	*Wagner*
Brandenburg Concerto No. 3	*Bach*
Symphonic Poem, *Don Juan*	*Strauss*
Concerto No. 3 *in C Minor for Pianoforte and*	
Orchestra	*Beethoven*
Introduction and Allegro for strings . .	*Elgar*
Scherzo and Finale from Symphony No. 5 *in*	
C Minor	*Beethoven*
Ride of the Valkyries	*Wagner*

The *Daily Telegraph* also sponsored the memorial concert on 4 March 1945, again adding a very large sum to the fund, which had now become the Henry Wood Memorial Fund. The programme, presented to a packed Royal Albert Hall, included Vaughan Williams's *Serenade to Music*. The sixteen solo singers were:

Soprano	*Contralto*
Mary Hamlin	Margaret Balfour
Stiles-Allen	Muriel Brunskill
Maggie Teyte	Astra Desmond
Eva Turner	Janet Howe

Tenor	*Bass*
Parry Jones	Norman Allin
Trefor Jones	Henry Cummings
Edward Reach	Roy Henderson
Henry Wendon	George Pizzey

The orchestras were the B.B.C. Symphony Orchestra, London Philharmonic Orchestra and the London Symphony Orchestra, directed severally by John Barbirolli (now Sir John), Sir Adrian Boult, and Basil Cameron.

In 1946 the *Daily Telegraph* again added several thousands to the Henry Wood Concert Hall Fund when they sponsored a performance of Beethoven's Mass in D at the Royal Albert Hall on 3 March, under the title of the Sir Henry Wood Birthday Concert, bringing to London the fine Huddersfield Choir. The B.B.C. Symphony Orchestra with soloists Joan Hammond, Gladys Ripley, Parry Jones, George Pizzey, were under the direction of Dr. Malcolm Sargent (now Sir Malcolm Sargent). Oscar Pulvermacher of the *Daily Telegraph* performed a miracle in those very difficult days in organizing transport and meals to and from Huddersfield for a choir of over three hundred.

Lord Horder, as chairman of the fund, gathered around himself an array of well-known musicians and friends and I well remember how delighted Henry was to find his old friend Lord Horder again championing his cause—just as he did in 1938, when he sat on Sir Robert Mayer's committee in commemoration of Henry's fiftieth year as a professional conductor.

It was very difficult to get money anywhere during the war days, with no opportunity of publicity, and that the fund eventually reached something in the neighbourhood of £70,000 gives a good account of Lord Horder's chairmanship. Some members of the committee regretted the decision to build a concert hall "when Queen's Hall is going to be rebuilt". That was in 1944, and to-day, a decade later, Queen's Hall remains a gaunt monument to Hitlerism, and there is still no Henry Wood Memorial.

The fund eventually closed with a sum of some £77,000. Following the suggestion put forward by Sir Adrian Boult,

Basil Cameron and Sir Malcolm Sargent, the government has agreed that this money will be directed to building a small hall within Queen's Hall when the latter is rebuilt. As mentioned earlier, this small hall will be known as the Henry Wood Rehearsal Hall. It has been agreed that it should be built to accommodate a full symphony orchestra and a choir of three hundred. Failing a completely new concert hall, I cannot think of a more fitting memorial to Henry Wood than a hall specially designed and reserved for orchestral rehearsals. We have nowhere in London at present in which to rehearse except the hall where the concert itself is to take place. But the hire of a hall only provides for one rehearsal on the day of the concert. Extra rehearsals can be obtained only by reserving the hall at set times on previous days, which frequently means that sufficient rehearsal time has to be sacrificed because of the high cost of booking concert halls on the additional day at the full hire charges.

After Henry's death, beside myself with grief and almost bereft of any feeling of life, I tried to interpret Henry's wishes. He had left no special directions or requests in his straightforward will. Two things I knew. One was that he disliked a burial ground or a garden of remembrance. The other, that he had one day, in passing, suggested that his ashes be scattered on the roof of Queen's Hall. The suggestion was made before Queen's Hall was destroyed and he had made no further reference to the subject.

Dr. Skeggs and his family gave me comfort and confidence to attend to immediate details. They made their home in Stevenage over to me and to the many friends who came to look their last on a dear colleague. So I took courage and made arrangements for friends and colleagues to travel from London. Sir Charles Newton—general manager of the L.N.E.R. (no British Railways then!)—whom we had met so often in Stevenage, made possible a special return train. Without his help this could not have been done in wartime.

Beautiful St. Mary's Church in Hitchin was filled with Henry's friends. The B.B.C. Symphony Orchestra were led by Paul Beard, the B.B.C. singers conducted by Leslie Woodgate. Sir Adrian Boult directed the *Adagio ma non troppo* from the Brandenburg Concerto No. 6 by Bach and Basil Cameron directed Chopin's Funeral March. Mr. Maurice Stretch, the organist of St. Mary's Church, played the *Adagio Cantabile* from Beethoven's Sonata Pathétique, and Dr. Thalben Ball played the lovely air from Handel's *Berenice* and Henry's arrangement of Handel's *Largo* in E. The service was conducted by the Rev. Hugh Matthews, rector of St. Marylebone, and the Rev. Roger Bagnall. The 23rd psalm, "The Lord is my shepherd", the anthem, "How lovely is thy dwelling-place", by Brahms, and the hymn, "Praise to the Holiest in the height", ending with Henry's favourite Sevenfold Amen, were sung very beautifully by the B.B.C. singers. Mr. B. E. Nicolls made it possible to hear this lovely music that day by giving his consent for the orchestra and singers to attend the service. Those dear singers told me many months afterwards that they could hardly sing for the grief in their hearts. It was a beautiful service and embraced all I knew Henry would have wished.

But where, where was I to bury his ashes?

Suddenly I knew, as if Henry himself had spoken: why, St. Sepulchre's Church, Holborn, London! I telephoned Elsie Newmarch to see the vicar on my behalf and ask him to give sanctuary to the ashes pending an ultimate decision. Later I met the vicar, Canon G. H. Salter, and Henry came to rest in the old London parish church where he had worshipped as a boy, played the organ, and listened as his parents sang in the choir.

Canon Salter had told me, when he said how much he wished Henry's remains should rest in the church: "I used to attend the Promenade Concerts when at Oxford, and from Henry Wood I learned most of my music."

Eventually the ashes, which had been given a temporary resting-place in a niche on the right of the altar awaiting faculty, were buried, faculty having been granted at the same time for a memorial window which I wished to place in the north of the chapel.

I found in Gerald E. R. Smith and that great painter, Frank O. Salisbury, not only artistic interest in the window but a co-operation of unusual and loving warmth in their affection for the man in whose memory the window was to be designed and erected. As for the finished work, I cannot do better than quote from Alec Robertson's wonderful description, given in the programme of the unveiling service on 26 April 1946:

"It is not, as is too often supposed, the purpose of a stained glass window to suffuse into the church a dim religious light, but rather to admit jewelled light. And not only to delight us with its colour, but, pre-eminently, to awaken the imagination of the beholder in telling its story. And in this memorial window, designed by Gerald E. R. Smith in collaboration with Frank O. Salisbury, and dedicated to Henry Joseph Wood in the name of musicians and friends of music, there can be found facts imaginatively presented, and meanings symbolically conveyed. At the top of the window, where shines the luminous figure of the crucified Saviour, light pours forth over the world, angels with trumpets announce peace on earth to men of good will, God's rainbow is set in the heavens.

"Any man who serves his art with the selfless devotion that Henry Wood brought to it bears a daily cross; and any man whose one desire it is to help others, fulfils the sense of Blake's words, 'Every act of kindness is a little death in the Divine Image'. We may in these two ways at once relate the message of the Cross at the top of the window, to its fulfilment in the lower panel. We see, in the left panel, the young Henry playing the organ. His father was principal tenor in the choir of the Church of St. Sepulchre for many years, he learnt to play the organ here under Dr. Lott, and he was in charge of the organ loft at the age of twelve. It is fitting that Henry Wood's ashes should be buried immediately beneath this memorial window, on the site where the organ once stood.

"In the complementary right-hand panel we see the beloved 'Henry J.' of the Promenade Concerts, the man who might have echoed the words of Keats: 'I have loved the principle of beauty in all things and the memory of great men.' And here along the length of this lower panel stand four of the great men of music, Bach and Handel, Byrd and Purcell. The medallion, surrounded by a laurel wreath, carries a verse written for it by the Poet Laureate: above it flowers one of the carnations which we all remember as part of Sir Henry's platform personality, below there is the painter's palette which, alone among the arts, challenged the conductor's baton in his affections. On the music scroll is written Stainer's Sevenfold Amen, in which Sir Henry found constant inspiration.

"These are the words within the medallion:

" 'At this Man's hand a million hearers caught
An echo of the Music without flaw
Whose endless joy is Heaven's only law
O Music-lovers, bless him in your thought.'
John Masefield.

"We will indeed, all of us, bless him in our thoughts, and, so doing, again raise our eyes to the Cross, the ideal self-sacrifice from which he drew his strength. It was Henry Wood's practice to read nightly in the New Testament; but in times of fatigue or stress he would open the Passion according to St. Matthew by John Sebastian Bach, the score he treasured most of all in the world, his deepest faith become music. In that music, he always found refreshment and repose.

"In the central part of the window, St. Cecilia, the patron saint of music, is seated with attendant angels at the organ. No proven historical fact connects her with music, but she is supposed according to tradition to have been found singing after the three days of her cruel martyrdom were passed: and, so singing, died.

"The Church has put into her mouth, in one of the vesperal antiphons, the lovely prayer *'Fiat cor immaculatum, ut non confundar'*.

"We remember, looking at this centre panel, Henry Wood's great desire for the revival in England of the Cecilian Festival —to which Purcell and Handel had contributed in the past— but we remember, above all, the man who lives on to inspire and encourage all lovers of music, present and to come."

As this window neared completion, I set about gathering

a committee whose members would, in their affection for Henry, assist in making a beautiful memory of the unveiling service. These friends of music included R. S. Thatcher (now Sir Reginald Thatcher), principal of the Royal Academy of Music, Julian Herbage, W. W. Thompson and Leslie Woodgate.

Quite by chance, on a journey to Manchester in October 1944, I met Sir William (later Lord) Jowitt, and, in speaking of Henry's great work for music and what a loss music had suffered, he told me that if at any time he could be of assistance in any way in Henry's cause, to ask it of him. Remembering this, I wrote to him asking if he would speak an appreciation when the memorial window was to be unveiled on 26 April 1946. As we know, Lord Jowitt came to St. Sepulchre's Church that day, and in that wonderfully beautiful voice of his said, as only he could say, the following words:

"The window which the Lord Mayor will shortly unveil commemorates the life-work of Sir Henry Wood. It is fitting that the window should be placed in this church, for here it was that some sixty-seven years ago, when a mere boy, he played the organ. Of all the transitory things in this transitory life, music born on the air and dying with the breath that utters it seems the most impermanent. The performer of music may go from triumph to triumph in his lifetime, but is often soon forgotten when he is dead. The laurels wither more quickly than do those of other arts. The composer of music may, if he be great enough, secure immortality on one condition, that is that he finds a performer to recreate anew for him the conceptions of his mind which he had recorded in signs that the musician can read and interpret. Such an interpreter was Henry Wood, for he continually recreated the great music of the past, but not only of the past, for he singled out the most promising things of the present and he created the future as he went along.

"Not only did he serve his day and generation: he created an *institution*, and in creating it he became an institution himself. In this country tradition preserves alive what time would cast into oblivion. Henry Wood established a tradition of orchestral music for the people. By creation of the Promenade Concerts he embodied that tradition in an institution which will not only keep his name in remembrance, but will carry on his work so that the generations that did not know him in the flesh will through him be brought to a knowledge of the great classics.

"With characteristic openness of mind he welcomed the new facilities offered by broadcasting and thus brought music to the humblest homes. We who knew him remember him not only for the work he did for the music of instruments but for the encouragement he gave to choral singing —the great triennial festivals of Birmingham, Norwich, Sheffield and the Crystal Palace were all served by him, and in them he enriched the English tradition of choral singing.

"But to-day I would not speak to you only of the musician, I would speak of the man: perhaps, indeed, the two are inseparable. He was intensely 'human' with all the strength and with all the frailties that the adjective implies: warm-hearted, generous, and affectionate. He possessed that rare quality of leadership, which made him at least as interested in another's success as he was in his own. Throughout his life he maintained the endearing quality of youth; full of enthusiasm, full of fun—'come on and enjoy yourself', he would say to a young artist facing the ordeal of an audience;

completely free from any form of snobbery; at ease in any company; no heavy solemnity; no academic pedantry. He had an unrivalled appeal to his audiences; he did everything with his whole talent and purpose, and throughout his life he constantly multiplied the company of the lovers of music; that is his great achievement. Those of us who knew him and listened to his music will see that his life's work was not done in vain.

> "For some there be that by due steps aspire
> To lay their just hands on that golden key
> That opes the palace of Eternity."

*　　　　*　　　　*

A very dear friend had introduced me to the Lord Mayor's secretary, for I had determined that Henry, so much a Londoner, should be so honoured; and the Lord Mayor of London, Sir Charles Davis, performed the unveiling ceremony. Music naturally played a large part in this unforgettably beautiful ceremony. The whole service was broadcast, and from all sides was acclaimed as very moving. Inside the church, Henry seemed very near—the lovely Vaughan Williams *Serenade to Music*; the Walton work, sung for the first time set to the Poet Laureate's words, was completely lovely and heard to perfection that day; especially heart-gripping was the *pianissimo* dying away in its sweet harmonies. This setting of the Poet Laureate's verses—both the words and the music had been written at my request—has never sounded so beautiful as on this first hearing in the crowded, hushed church, and will never be forgotten by those present, and by the vast listening public.

The service was taken by the Very Reverend W. R. Matthews, Dean of St. Paul's, and the Vicar of St. Sepulchre's

Church, the Reverend G. H. Salter. The processional hymn and anthem were sung by the St. Paul's Cathedral Choir, directed by Dr. John Dykes Bower, and the Westminster Abbey Choir, directed by Dr. William McKie (now Sir William). The B.B.C. Singers and Chorus directed by Mr. Leslie Woodgate sang Sir William Walton's work, set to verses by the Poet Laureate, "Where does the uttered music go?" *Serenade to Music* was sung by Stiles-Allen, Elena Danieli, Mary Hamlin, Eva Turner, Muriel Brunskill, Janet Howe, Emelie Hooke, Mary Jarred, Jan van der Gucht, Heddle Nash, Walter Widdop, Henry Wendon, Trevor Anthony, Owen Brannigan, Henry Cummings and Roy Henderson. The *Trumpet Voluntary* by Purcell-Wood was played by Ernest Hall. The B.B.C. Symphony Orchestra, leader Paul Beard, and the London Symphony Orchestra, leader George Stratton, were directed by Basil Cameron. At my request, The Musicians' Benevolent Fund organized the ceremony in the name of musicians and lovers of music.

CHAPTER 13

Musical Discipline and Musical Democracy

When Henry died in 1944 many of his old colleagues of the Queen's Hall Orchestra wrote to me, including such fine artists as Eugene Goossens, Emile Ferrier, Henri de Buscher, Alfred Kastner, Jacques Renard, Warwick Evans and others too numerous to mention.

It is interesting to read their letters because, if you have read *My Life of Music*, you may think the members of the early Queen's Hall Orchestra would retain unhappy memories of those hard-working days and the diligent young workman directing operations. Not a bit of it; one and all cherish those days of very stern disciplined training. They hold nothing but nostalgic regard and gratitude for their old chief. When in 1940 John Barbirolli was in America, he wrote to Henry sending a photograph he had had specially taken after finding old friends of the Queen's Hall Orchestra gathered under his direction at the Hollywood Bowl. The letter said:

"Whilst conducting at the Hollywood Bowl this season I discovered that three old and very distinguished members of your own Queen's Hall Orchestra were still playing there. You will of course remember your old friends Emile Ferrier ('cello), Henri de Buscher (oboe), Alfred Kastner (harp). My wife, also with me in Hollywood, you will remember too, having played first oboe for you as Evelyn Rothwell; so that we found ourselves five old members of the Queen's Hall Orchestra suddenly thrown together in California. We had a grand talk about 'the good old days', of yourself and the work we had done with you."

Later Henri de Buscher wrote:

"I was the first oboe player in the Queen's Hall Orchestra from 1904 to 1913, under the able direction of Sir Henry Wood, then Mr. Henry Wood. I look back on those nine years as the most pleasant and inspiring ones of my life. The growth of musical appreciation in those years was amazing, and most certainly the way Sir Henry built up the programmes and educated audiences to know and like both classic and modern music. . . . In all my long experience as a symphonic performer, I have never known a conductor to accomplish so much in so short a time. He had the most practical and methodical method of working. For instance, he never left parts of new compositions to be corrected during rehearsal. He himself did that beforehand, even working at nights over them. He achieved the most outstanding performances of great works in my recollection. Sir Henry Wood was the most genial and the most beloved of all conductors I have ever played under, and I hope this desire of his heart for a new Hall of Music in London will soon materialize, and that it will be a monument to this truly great man."

Another orchestra player, the 'cellist Warwick Evans, wrote:

"Nothing I can say would be worthy enough, and no hall that has ever been built will be good enough for dear

'Old Timber'—no disrespect, just a lovable term among the 'lads'. How *can* I write anything worthy of dear old Henry? I was his first 'cello player for many years, and I owe almost everything to him. His fine enthusiasm for work was a great example to all artists."

How happy Henry would have been to read all the affectionate tributes from colleagues the world over, especially those from players he had worked with and loved in the hard, grinding days of his Queen's Hall Orchestra. Here is yet another, from Jacques Renard, who followed, I think, W. H. Squire as leader of the 'cellos:

"Although nearly half a century ago, my impression of the first concert of my first Promenade Concert season is still very vivid. In those days it was the custom, after the rest of the orchestra was seated, for the principal players to walk on to the concert stage one by one to receive an ovation from the audience on the opening night of the season. When my turn came, being a stranger and having replaced a favourite in the orchestra, I walked to my seat in dead silence facing what looked to me like a sea of white straw sailor hats—it being the month of August.

"After Sir Henry made his bow, the concert started with Rossini's overture to *William Tell*. As is well known, this work opens with a solo quartet of four 'cellos, depicting the sunrise on the mountains, the first two bars being played by the first 'cellist alone. At the finish of the work, a great favourite with the public, there was of course thunderous applause.

"Sir Henry, instead of turning round to acknowledge this applause, stepped down from his podium, walked over to

my seat, shook me by the hand and made me rise to share
the plaudits with him. This was the gracious and subtle way
of Sir Henry to introduce his new first 'cellist to the Promenade audience.

"Further impressions of the man were the cordial relations existing between him and all the members of the
orchestra. His passion for work was insatiable. He knew
every score from A to Z, whether old or new music, including the works of many young British composers, when the
rehearsals started. His reading of scores was phenomenal.
I remember the morning when five principal string players
gathered in his studio for the purpose of the co-ordination
of bow-markings in their parts of Strauss's *Symphonia Domes-
tica*. Sir Henry sat at the piano with the huge score in front
of him from which he filled in all the harmonies, etc., while
we played, which is some stunt with the various clefs for
the different wind instruments.

"As an organizer he had no peer, whether it was a Sheffield or Norwich Festival, or making up the programmes
for the Promenade Concerts. The allotting of time for rehearsing the numbers, including those of the soloists, with
only three rehearsals for six concerts a week; all was fixed
in advance for the whole season of ten weeks, and every
piece timed for the three-hour concerts.

"As an accompanist of soloists, either with the orchestra
or on the piano, he was unsurpassed. He could anticipate
the intentions of the artist. As I played many concertos
under his conductorship I know this by experience. . . .
My connections with the Queen's Hall Orchestra under the
congenial direction of Sir Henry were the happiest years of
my life."

Thus the musicians of those days bore Henry no grudge for his blue pencil or his discipline. They write during these comparatively easy years for orchestral players—when the memory of the hard grind of the early Queen's Hall Orchestra might be recalled as anything but pleasant—with only happy memories.

Henry, if he were here to listen to them would repeat what he so often said to me:

"Ah, my dear, the men of those days were of the highest executant standard built on the frugal upbringing of musicians of that time—work, work, work; that is why I was so completely understood and so fortunate."

Henry often recalled in later life the hard road musicians had had to travel in those years. In more recent times, when some seemingly trivial grouse from the orchestra would come his way through the orchestral manager, he would respond:

"My goodness, they should have had to struggle as we were obliged to do, no quick tube trains home, no cheap meals provided, no canteens, few if any grants for students' welfare, and *very* few chances of getting a seat in an orchestra (and only a couple in London then), much less a hearing as a solo artist unless endowed with a very high standard of efficiency; there was no room for any but those of the highest grade."

Henry was unquestionably in advance of his time when he instituted orchestral discipline and a regular régime; for him nothing could prosper unless the field for action was planned and made ready in every small detail. Some of the old orchestral players used occasionally to curse him for his punctiliousness, for he seemed to them to pay an absurdly fastidious attention to minor details. But, as time went on, they learnt to reverence this characteristic. A rehearsal, to Henry, was in many ways far more important than a public performance, and in his early Queen's Hall days this led to a certain confusion of ideals. Some players would not, and could not, align themselves to his utter sincerity of purpose. Hence, such practices as the locking-out of late-comers, and other reforms, led to much private dislike of the shock-headed, bearded young man of twenty-six. All this Henry himself related in *My Life of Music*. But we see, from the letters published in these pages, how the artists of the orchestra came to cherish warm and affectionate memories of him just the same.

All true orchestral musicians now know how right Henry was and, looking back over more than fifty years of H.J.W., they realize that the position they enjoy to-day is derived from the efforts made by him in those pioneer days to win not only the best artistic results but higher status and prestige for English orchestral musicians.

His discipline was for the definite good of music and it created as time went on a standard which has come to be recognized among musicians and managements everywhere and which is welcomed by the really good professional players.

Some time ago the daily papers announced that several key players had resigned because a 'rehearsal time-sheet' was instituted. One of them had remarked:

"We should not be asked to 'clock in'. Our permanent conductor knows us and would not ask this of us."

But to sacrifice essential discipline because it interferes with an easy-going, friendly relationship between a conductor and his orchestra leads to one inevitable result. Possibly a Beethoven symphony or a Tchaikovsky programme is listed for rehearsal, and in an 'easy-going' orchestra the player, feeling secure of a 'let-off' for such repertoire works, will take time off for private interests at the expense of adequate rehearsal. And don't we hear the results in some of our concert halls and over the air sometimes!

It was not so with Henry Wood. How easily he might have saved himself during the annual Promenade Concerts. All the players knew his sure beat so well that purely repertoire works could have been programmed without rehearsal. But never would he eschew rehearsal of an old war-horse. If any work missed rehearsal it was because some unexpected problem arose—often the time-stealing enthusiasm, difficult to curb, of a composer-conductor running through his composition before a first performance.

From the outset of his career that orderliness which characterized his whole mind found that regulations, plain markings, notes—all and everything that could diminish the risk of the unexpected during a rehearsal—were an absolute necessity when dealing with a large number of orchestral musicians, if ideal results were to be attained.

This was much disliked, in fact ridiculed, by some. From the start his players tended to resent his steel-like demands— and so some players, entirely through their own dislike of discipline (always a means to an end where Henry was concerned), never knew the warm and very human heart of Henry Wood. To be happy with Henry his orderliness of mind had to be understood; but to understand meant an understanding, too, of his artistic ideals, his utter absorption in his work. In the very early days most of the musicians of the orchestra had become accustomed to older men on the rostrum, such as Manns or Richter, whose direction was easy-going as they attained years. Few other conductors counted in England at that time, where there were no really permanent orchestras. To have this youthful Englishman—a Londoner born and bred, at that—laying down a new law in the name of music was irritably challenged, often quite openly, and there was a very real and personal struggle for a while.

Those who protested foolishly erected a barrier between themselves and a young man who had a heart of gold and a mind free from that dross which muddied the make-up of some musicians. He had also—as those who took the trouble soon found out—a sympathy and human understanding rarely found in one with an ideal as fixed as his. What was that ideal? To bring music to a great public and bring it in such an impeccable manner as to win the untutored thousands; yet, at the same time, to satisfy his own exacting and sensitive musicianship.

His old friend Rosa Newmarch, in an article published at the time the B.B.C. first took over the Promenade Concerts, said:

"As long ago as 1904 I wrote of him (Henry Wood): 'His greatest service to his art and his country lies in the fact that he has liberated music from its exclusive sphere and offered it to the people.' Time has confirmed this assertion and proved that consciously and subconsciously he has always been pressing towards the realization of the broadest democratic ideal in his art. The word 'democratic' is used here in its unvulgarized sense as meaning that Henry Wood has a natural perception of what 'befits the people' aesthetically considered."

Methodically, with orderly determination and by insisting on the highest quality, he brought the world's best music to the English people, and for two whole generations the Promenade Concerts have symbolized all that is best in musical enjoyment to immense, enthusiastic but now educated audiences from every walk of life.

CHAPTER 14

Henry Wood and Russia

HENRY WOOD'S EARLY interest in the music of Russia began with the first performance in England of Tchaikovsky's opera *Eugene Onegin*, which he produced and directed at His Majesty's Theatre, London, in 1892 when he was twenty-three!

It was an interest, full of understanding and sympathy, which lasted all his life. It influenced both his private and his musical life, for Henry's first wife, whom he married in July 1898, was the Russian Princess Olga Ouroussoff, who shared his life in what Henry himself called a 'perfect union' for eleven years until her untimely death in 1909. The shock of that bereavement, rendering life—again in Henry's own words —"devoid of all meaning", together with the loss of Olga's guidance, was a tragic blow in his life.

It is not generally known that Henry declined the suggestion of a knighthood while Olga was alive because he said he could offer her no greater honour than she had conferred on him by marriage, since she was a lady of title. That is why it was not until 1911 that he accepted the honour.

Musically Henry maintained his connection with Russia, and many new works by Russian composers figured annually in first performances in England. This continued up to 1944, when he directed Shostakovich's Eighth Symphony on 13 July.

The Russians, irrespective of régime, did not fail to appreciate the interest and understanding shown in their works—and no nation was more forward with tributes than Soviet Russia when Henry celebrated his seventy-fifth birthday in 1944.

The members of the musical section of VOKS—the Soviet

Society of Cultural Relations with Foreign Countries—sent a long, heart-warming telegram to Henry on the occasion of that birthday and the Promenade jubilee. It said:

"With feelings of heartfelt joy and deepest respect Soviet musicians mark the happy occasion of your seventy-fifth birthday and the fiftieth anniversary of your famous Promenade Concerts. Your name as indefatigable exponent of music, as educator cultivating public taste for music, as inspired interpreter of musical works written by the world's greatest composers, is well known to and highly esteemed by musicians of the Soviet Union.

"We also equally value your profound appreciation of Russian art and Russian music. We are aware of your inestimable efforts in acquainting Englishmen with the musical soul of our country.

"In these days of war against Hitlerism, in these days of ordeal and struggle, never for a moment have you ceased your service to art. Nazis wantonly destroyed the historic Queen's Hall, but the Promenade Concerts continue in London and still draw thousands of music lovers.

"In these grim days the significance of music has acquired a greater import than ever before.

"Across seas and land we extend you our hand in firm and friendly greetings.

"We warmly greet you on the occasion of your glorious golden and diamond jubilees and wish you many, many years of good health, good cheer, and creative success."

In addition there were many tributes and lengthy articles in the Soviet Press describing Henry's work and career.

The All-Union Society for Cultural Relations with Foreign Countries also held an evening meeting in Moscow in March

1944 in honour of Henry's seventy-fifth birthday. The assembly was opened by the VOKS president, V. Klemenov, and the meeting was attended by the British Minister Plenipotentiary, Mr. John Balfour, the composer Prokofiev, and leading musicians and professors. An address of greeting was delivered by Professor A. Alexandrov. Dmitri Shostakovich, who was not able to attend as he was giving a concert, sent word asking that his best wishes be passed on to Henry, adding:

> "We Soviet composers cherish a profound respect and admiration for the activities of Sir Henry Wood, who is a great musician, patriot and friend of Russian music."

Another message came from the staff of the Scriabin Museum in Moscow who sent their "best congratulations to a great artist, the first conductor of *Prometeus* in London."

In addition to these and other messages, Russian musicians sent a letter of congratulations and greetings to Henry in the form of a beautifully inscribed and illuminated parchment. The text of the letter is in Russian and it was signed by the composers Serge Prokofiev, Alexander Alexandrov, Alexander Krein, Alexander Tzfasman, conductor Alexander Gauk, pianist Emil Gilels, composer Samuel Feinberg, conductor Nikolai Anosov and composer Dmitri Kabalevsky among others.

Nor did the Maiskys, now in Moscow, forget Henry's birthday. Henry was delighted to receive a cable from them:

> "Heartiest congratulations your seventy-five anniversary. We highly appreciate your valuable work which so much contributed to the cultural rapprochement between our two peoples and wish you every success in its continuation. Many happy returns. Greetings to your wife. Agnes and Ivan Maisky."

One has grown accustomed in recent years to treating everything, especially organized tributes from official Soviet groups, as part of the propaganda of the cold war. In those days, of course, Russia was our ally. Doubtless Russians do not drop in to the local post office and dispatch a cable to a citizen of a foreign land without a thought about the views of the authorities. But these tributes, as their real warmth and the understanding they showed of Henry's musical work indicated, were, I am certain, completely sincere and came from the heart. They were tributes from musicians to a musician linked to them by a much finer bond than those that political propagandists deal with—a love of beautiful music.

Of course, these Russian tributes were far from being the only ones that showered upon Henry from all directions in the closing months of his life—the total of the messages and greetings was too great to enumerate here.

One, however, from quite a different source, I cannot omit. Like Henry's link with the Russian composers, it was something that spanned the whole length of his career. Bernard Shaw, as a young, red-headed critic, fully appreciated what Henry was doing for music—and half a century later he summed up his feelings in a glowing tribute:

"Only those who, like myself, had to act as critics of London music fifty years ago can possibly appreciate what we owe to Henry Wood. Younger connoisseurs have heard and seen him conduct; but they have not suffered from his early contemporaries the pre-Richter conductors. And they do not know, and would not believe me if I told them, what the Promenade Concerts were like at Covent Garden in the eighteen-eighties. It was Wood who dragged British orchestral music alive out of that abyss. And after a life-

work which would have staled and worn out anyone but
Wood, when the wireless gave him an audience of millions
to play to in the Albert Hall with a splendidly full band,
he rose to the occasion and surpassed himself in performances which crowned him as a master of his art and the
peer of the greatest of his European rivals.

> "G. Bernard Shaw,
>
> "New Year, 1944."

Bernard Shaw wrote that in his own hand, and that, too,
clearly came from the heart. There were few, like Shaw, who
could cast their minds back over so many years, tracing out
the progress step by step—and with the accumulated knowledge of decades accurately place the credit where it was due.
A musical criticism from Shaw's pen in his later years, after
he had succeeded and become world-famous as a dramatist,
was unusual—and this tribute he sent Henry must be something of a rarity. And it has, too, a stamp of real authority,
real musical understanding, upon it.

Shaw was always a great admirer of Henry's work. On one
occasion, having heard a performance in the Queen's Hall of
Beethoven's "Leonora No. 2", he wrote a post-card saying:

> "That was one of your greatest triumphs.
>
> "You actually convinced me that Beethoven, when he
> substituted No. 3, spoiled a colossal tragic overture just to
> make it slick. [Not all musicians would agree with this!]
>
> "No conductor ever did this before.
>
> "Note the hour and date.
>
> > "G. Bernard Shaw,
> >
> > "6.45 p.m., 10. 7. 1942."

On 17 October 1941 Shaw had also written a long, amusing post-card complaining that in big Beethoven *tuttis* where chords were supported by brass and upper strings the moving bass was often inaudible. He pointed out that the bass part was heard much better when he played the overtures as piano duets with his sister, and naïvely suggests that the passages should be re-scored and the bass doubled with five-valve trombones or an ophicleide or bass saxophones (which he refers to as wood wind). He stated that Elgar agreed with his suggestions. (It is possible that Elgar found it a very tiring form of entertainment to attempt to disagree with Bernard Shaw!) As Shaw stated in his writing to Henry that the ophicleide "was as flexible as a piccolo", students are not advised to take too seriously his suggestions for re-orchestration.

He supplemented this with another post-card dated the same day:

"I have just remembered that a bass saxophone (if the animal is not fabulous) must be a metal instrument; so Coates may be right. If so, it suggests a modern ophicleide. As late as Gluck the violins were doubled by oboes as the cellos still are by bassoons. Why not double the big basses by saxophones? The old cornetto, supposed to be obsolete, has been rediscovered by the Salvation Army as the soprano cornet. It needs a good bit to play it; but it is not vulgar like the cornet, and ought to be used in the orchestra for high cantabile effects as a change from the oboe and violin.

"Excuse my bothering you with this: it is only to correct my slip in calling the saxophone wood wind.

"G. B. S."

CHAPTER 15

The Music Plays On

It REMAINED FOR me, heartbroken as I was, to carry out Henry's wishes to the utmost of my power—to secure so far as I was able the performance of those works on which Henry had set his heart during the wartime days but had been unable to direct because of hostilities.

With that aim in mind I gathered a committee around me, and in August 1946 the Henry Wood Concert Society was formed. Sir Arnold Bax kindly consented to act as president and Lord Horder as vice-president. The committee itself included Julian Herbage, vice-chairman, Norman Allin, Dr. W. Greenhouse Allt, principal of the Trinity College of Music, W. W. Thompson (who later resigned), G. P. Mead (hon. treasurer), Sir Frank Newson-Smith, Leslie Regan, Sir Reginald Thatcher, Leslie Woodgate, Dorothy Wood (hon. secretary). Sir Arnold Bax died last year, and the society mourned a great friend. We are honoured afresh in Sir Arthur Bliss having graciously agreed to accept the presidentship—Sir Arthur—as was Sir Arnold—is Master of the Queen's Music.

The main activity of the society is to sponsor concerts and to devote itself to causes and services which advance the art of music and extend its appreciation—especially to those causes and services which Henry Wood had most at heart.

And it was with this in mind that I gathered together my committee, persons who would revere Henry's memory and join in bringing about performances Henry would have taken delight in.

187

The Henry Wood Concert Society has, despite the many difficulties of sponsoring concerts in the post-war period, when orchestra and other fees have doubled since Henry died ten years ago, and despite certain times when there has been almost a glut of performances of various kinds, succeeded in carrying out many of Henry's musical ambitions.

One, in particular, I know would have given him the deepest satisfaction—the 1949 Elgar Festival, when ten Elgar concerts were given within three weeks, eight of which took place at the Royal Albert Hall. Never before had such a festival been held for Elgar—indeed for any British composer. Her Majesty the Queen (now Queen Elizabeth the Queen Mother) honoured the society with her presence at the opening concert of the festival, and in Henry's name I was privileged to present to Her Majesty John Barbirolli (whose knighthood later gave satisfaction to us all). Undoubtedly this vast, comprehensive festival, covering as it did the whole output of the composer's works, gave the musical public an unforgettable opportunity to enjoy Elgar in a way that has not occurred before or since. No other composer figured in any of those ten programmes. How happy that achievement would have made Henry!

In the same way, and in the same spirit, the society carried out other wishes expressed by Henry during the war —performances of *Parsifal*, Mahler's Second and Eighth Symphonies, Dvorak's *Stabat Mater* and other worthwhile works. In its first years the society commissioned works by Bax, Berkeley, Murrill and Walton.

We were also very happy to be able to give a first appearance to John Heddle Nash, a young baritone from the Guildhall School of Music. How delighted Henry would have been to welcome the son of his old friend, Heddle Nash!

Henry had nursed another ambition, often voiced, to see

the Day of St. Cecilia, patron saint of musicians, revived. He looked for musicians to join hands to kindle the fire of equality in the arts, in which poor old music has always been the Cinderella. As long ago as 1936 he had quietly pressed the project among colleagues but nothing came of it at that time.

Later he suggested to the B.B.C. that the Corporation might lend its immense influence and associate itself with a revival of the custom of commemorating 22 November, St. Cecilia's Day. He argued that music and musicians should find equal public acknowledgement with the art of painting and that the only direct way to do this was to establish an annual banquet to which leaders in every walk of life might be invited to meet musicians at home. Such a social gathering was impossible, of course, in wartime.

Nevertheless, he went to work with a view to commissioning a musical work every year in the name of St. Cecilia, until such time as this could be augmented by the banquet he envisaged. In 1943 the B.B.C. invited Sir Arnold Bax to write such a composition. His violin concerto was the outcome. Henry spent many hours studying the score and, as was his custom, eventually saw for himself that the orchestral parts were correct in every detail. After this short-lived achievement, the saint's day was again in danger of becoming forgotten—despite Henry's enthusiasm whenever he could find an interested ear.

"I cannot understand musicians," he declared. "You would think they would be only too anxious to team up for an annual festival, or whatever we should call it." He had suggested making an appeal over the radio for the Musicians' Benevolent Fund on the Sunday evening before or after St. Cecilia's Day, making the appeal in her name. He had noted this in his own handwriting in his 1944 desk diary. This page, which I gave to the Musicians' Benevolent Fund, is now framed and hangs in the Fund's reception office at Carlos Place.

Eventually the first revival of the St. Cecilia's Day celebration was undertaken by the Musicians' Benevolent Fund, and a service was held on 22 November 1946. This was undoubtedly the outcome of the lovely unveiling ceremony of the memorial window earlier the same year. The St. Cecilia's Day service was held in St. Sepulchre's Church and was broadcast.

The *Daily Herald* sponsored the 1946 and 1947 St. Cecilia celebrations in a lavish manner, though in a style ordained by Canon Salter and the committee of the Musicians' Benevolent Fund. In accordance with Henry's original suggestion, several new works were commissioned and received their first performance at a concert given in the Albert Hall in the evening. Unfortunately the committee seemed to believe that only British music should appear in the name of St. Cecilia, despite Henry's hope that such concerts would represent music of every sphere of thought and nationality. St. Cecilia is the patron saint of all musicians everywhere.

It is undeniable that a purely British programme is no sure box-office or public attraction. The St. Cecilia's Day celebrations would flourish and gather an annual public in the name of music and musicians by embracing great works of international repute and international artists.

Now, when all is said of his life in *My Life of Music* (covering the years 1869-1938) and this appendix (1938-1944) Henry Wood lives on in his creation, the Henry Wood Promenade Concerts, which celebrate this year their diamond jubilee in the safe hands of Sir Malcolm Sargent with Basil Cameron retaining a part. John Hollingsworth has done splendid work as an associate conductor during the past four years, and certainly justified his position when Sir Malcolm was taken ill early in the 1951 season. He then took charge of the programmes. I recall how well he directed always and was especially acclaimed for his performance of Elgar's No. 1 Symphony. There is no doubt that with Sir Malcolm Henry's tradition is safe—for many years, we hope. I know that in all he undertakes reverence for Henry's child is his cherished determination.

I cannot help recalling a letter Sir Malcolm wrote to Henry in 1943, shortly before Henry's seventy-fifth birthday:

> "I shall always be grateful to you for having given me my first opportunity of conducting in London and for the continued inspiration your work has been to me to endeavour to follow in your footsteps.
>
> "I only hope that at seventy-five I shall be doing as good work for England as you are doing, and be as much held in honour by the discerning ones."

This diamond jubilee of the Henry Wood Promenade Concerts is a landmark without parallel in music-making anywhere in the world. Henry would be grateful (as we all are) to the B.B.C. for the manner in which they continue to sponsor these concerts—especially their determination to afford adequate rehearsals in spite of the always rising costs. Since Henry's death the B.B.C. not only honoured Henry's memory in each successive season of Promenade Concerts, but have never missed an opportunity of paying tribute to his work among themselves, and are now giving annually a Henry Wood Birthday Concert on a date as near 3 March as possible.

Sixty years, sixty seasons sweeping by packed with good things, new works, fine performances of repertoire works, an army of soloists including many famous names. Season after season, for two whole generations, young enthusiasts without deep pockets to pay for their musical pleasures have thronged to listen to the orchestras and soloists giving of their best. How wonderfully, too, over this span of years, have the enthusiastic audiences responded in their gratitude! What an institution to be proud of, this creation of Robert Newman and Henry! What a national glory!

Henry, by his determination and hard work, by his suffering and fighting—especially in those difficult days of 1939-40—made this diamond jubilee possible.

We have come a long way since the early struggles. In the fifty-ninth consecutive year of the Proms—1953—there were five orchestras and six conductors engaged, and at least two rehearsals for every concert. For so many years Henry, and only Henry, was willing and able to perform the gargantuan task alone.

I was touched when, after the concert on 5 August 1953 at which Sir Malcolm Sargent directed a vivid and beautifully treated performance of Richard Strauss's *Ein Heldenleben*, I reminded Malcolm that the previous performance of this work at a Prom had been on 31 August 1939, directed by Henry the day before war closed us down. "Ah," Malcolm said when I congratulated him on his rendering of the work. "What wouldn't old Henry have given to have all the rehearsals I am allowed for such works?"

And that is the manner of his thought during his work each year of helping Henry's baby to keep young. I know Henry would be the first to thank him and the B.B.C., and would be comforted to visualize the future of the Henry Wood Promenade Concerts.

So, in that spirit, we may look forward to the next years of the beloved Proms.